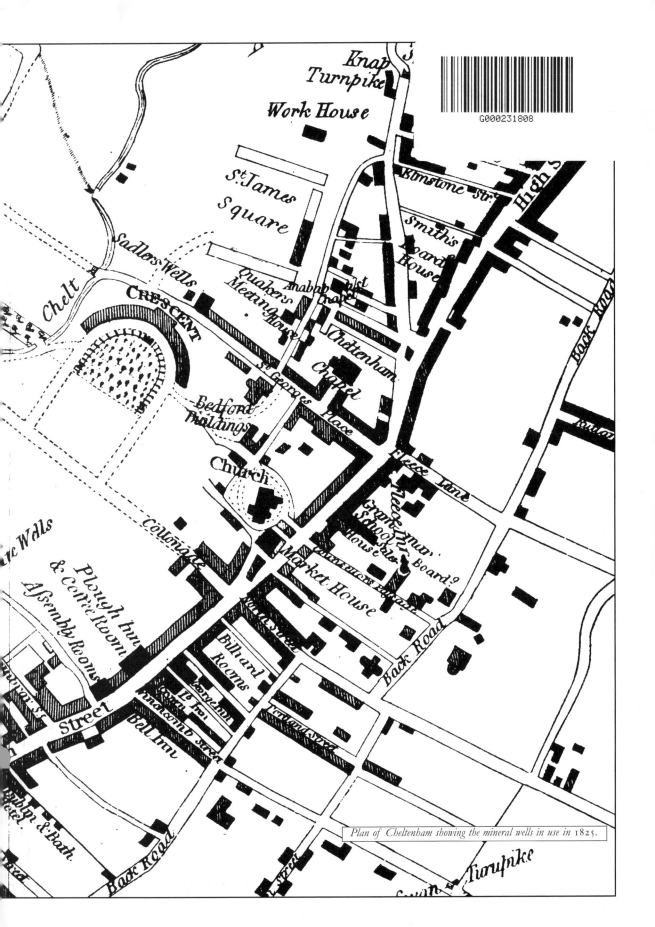

Knap
Turnpike
Work House
St James Square
Sadlers Wells
CRESCENT
Chelt
Quakers Meeting House
Bedford Buildings
St George's Place
Church
Cheltenham Chapel
Blenstone Str
High S
Smith's Board House
Fleece Lane
Grammar School House
Board?
Back Road
Colonnade
Plough Inn & Coffee Room Assembly Rooms
Market House
Billiard Rooms
Bell Inn
Street
Back Road
Back Road
Turnpike

Plan of Cheltenham showing the mineral wells in use in 1825.

CHELTENHAM
A History

A view of Lansdown Terrace by M.D Eichbaum c.1840. Some artistic licence has been used here as Christ Church cannot be seen from this point in Malvern Road.

CHELTENHAM

A History

Sue Rowbotham
and Jill Waller

Phillimore

2004

Published by
PHILLIMORE & CO. LTD
Shopwyke Manor Barn, Chichester, West Sussex, England

© Sue Rowbotham and Jill Waller, 2004

ISBN 1 86077 316 8

Printed and bound in Great Britain by
THE CROMWELL PRESS
Trowbridge, Wiltshire

Contents

List of Illustrations

Frontispiece: Lansdown Terrace, by M.D. Eichbaum *c*.1840.

Acknowledgements

The authors would like to thank the following institutions and individuals who kindly supplied illustrations and/or permission to use them in this book: Bristol and Gloucestershire Archaeological Society, 127 (*BGAS Transactions,* vol. 36, p.288); Michael Charity, 151; Cheltenham Art Gallery and Museum, frontispiece, 10, 11, 22, 24, 30, 31, 39, 43, 45, 50, 56, 63, 65, 91, 97, 102, 109, 113, 117, 125, 129, 136, 137, 143, 151, 152, 153; Cheltenham Civic Society, 96; Cheltenham Ladies' College, 4; Cheltenham Reference Library, Local Studies Centre, 22; Vic Cole and Martin Edwards, 94; Cotswold Archaeological Trust / John Lewis Partnership, 13, 14; GCHQ, 145, 146; Gloucester Library, 2, 15; *Gloucestershire Echo*, 143; David Kemish, 32, 40, 57; Lisa Lavery, 5, 26, 28, 133, 134, 154, 155; Tim Macaire, 138; Dave Martin, 150; Mary Nelson, 67; Geoff North and Elaine Heasman, jacket illustration, 99, 119; the Religious Society of Friends in Britain, 63; Dr A.G. Scott Langley, 105; Terry Sims, 90; John Whitaker, 139, 140.

Other illustrations have been taken from sources in the authors' own collections, including Davies, H., *View of Cheltenham in its Past and Present State* (1843), Griffith, S.Y., *Griffith's New Historical Description of Cheltenham and its Vicinity* (1826), Johnson, G.P., *New Historical and Pictorial Cheltenham and County of Gloucester Guide* (1846) and Rowe, George, *Rowe's Illustrated Cheltenham Guide* (1845). Every effort had been made to contact copyright holders, and we apologise if any have been missed.

The authors would especially like to thank Dr Steven Blake, of Cheltenham Art Gallery and Museum, not only for suggesting that they should write the book in the first place, but also for his patient guidance and advice, and for allowing them to roam freely through the museum resources. The authors are also indebted to Vic Cole, Mick Kippin and John Whitaker for their expert advice, and to Molly Walker for her skilled proofreading and comma-pruning.

Thanks are also due to Cheltenham Local History Society members who have shared their knowledge in the society's journal over the past 21 years, enhancing our understanding of the history of the town.

The authors are grateful for the time, information and expertise generously given by the following: Roger Beacham, Kath Boothman and Janet Mann (Cheltenham Ladies' College), Mike Clarke, Mike Grindley, Ann-Rachael Harwood, George and

Ailsa Howarth, Tony Hudson and Erica Smiter, Brian and Sue Jenner, Roger Jones, Richard and the late Jean Lacock, Lisa Lavery, Nick Lawrence, Christine Leighton (Cheltenham College), Tim Macaire, Peter and Moni Newman, Di Ryley, Terry Sims, Dr A.G. Scott Langley, Krys Waller, Martin Watts and Pete Moore (Cotswold Archaeological Trust), and George Wood. Finally, of course, the authors much appreciate the co-operation of their long-suffering families, whose understanding and support has made the research and writing of this book possible.

ONE

Before Records Began

Cheltenham lies at the foot of the Cotswold scarp, where the valley of the River Chelt meets the Severn Vale, sheltered from north and east winds by the surrounding hills. The main geology of the area consists of Jurassic deposits of Lias clays and Inferior Oolite limestone. The famous saline spa waters of Cheltenham, first noticed in 1716, originate from the underlying Lower Lias clay. Common minerals, such as magnesium and sodium salts, impregnate the saline waters, which led to many varieties of spa water being offered to visitors, each supposedly possessing different curative properties. In fact, unlike most other spa towns, Cheltenham never had a single concentrated centre for drinking the waters, and no other English spa has offered so many different types of mineral water. Some of the saline wells were sunk to a depth of 100 feet or more, only to yield less than 100 gallons a day. At the height of the fashion for spa water the presence of a saline well was a selling point for property. An 1813 advertisement for the sale of Alstone Lawn, a large mansion on the corner of Gloucester Road and Alstone Lane, proudly boasted 'besides a good supply of fresh

1 *View across Cheltenham from the roof of Pittville Pump Room, c.1835. Sheltered by the Cotswold hills, the local microclimate proved attractive to ex-colonials, who settled in the town.*

2 *Upper Alstone Mill in the 1950s, one of several medieval mill sites on the River Chelt. (Photograph by G.M. Davis.)*

deep, yielded about 200,000 gallons of fresh water daily. When the Cheltenham College Baths opened in 1880, about 33,000 gallons of fresh water were pumped daily into the swimming pool from wells on the site.

The Lower Lias clay reaches a depth of 300 metres in the Cheltenham and Gloucester area. The blue clay was laid down in a muddy sea 170-180 million years ago, and fossil ammonites and 'Devil's Toenails' (*Gryphaea*, an extinct oyster) are frequently found. But this was the Jurassic age of the dinosaur; a fossil Ichthyosaur, *Temnodontosaurus platyodon*, was unearthed in Malvern Road in 1899, while digging the foundations for the Ladies' College boarding house, Glenlee. Such a complete specimen is a rare find, and this one, measuring 14 feet, was displayed in the school museum until August 1917 when it was loaned to the town museum. Returned to the Ladies' College in July 1932, the fossil has since been 'lost'. Recently the school acquired a smaller ichthyosaur specimen that has been restored for display.

Spring and soft Water, there is a well of excellent Saline Water on the Premises'.

Overlying the Lower Lias clay are thick drifts of quartzose sand, known as Cheltenham Sand, thought to have blown in from the Midlands during dry glacial periods and been redeposited by water action. This sand is between six metres and 15 metres thick under central Cheltenham, producing a light, well-drained soil which, being easily cultivated, would have proved attractive to early settlers. The original settlement areas in Cheltenham, and in the surrounding hamlets of Alstone, Arle and Charlton Kings, coincide with these sandy deposits. In places the River Chelt tumbles over hard bands of clayey limestone, products of the erosion of the Cotswold hills. The waterfalls formed by these breaks in the slope dictated the siting of mills in the Middle Ages, including Barrett's Mill and Sandford Mill. Until the 20th century shallow wells sunk in the Cheltenham Sand provided fresh water supplies. These could yield surprisingly large amounts; the well near the Lido in Sandford Park, although only 24 feet

3 *Cheltenham Corporation Waterworks staff preparing their annual supper at the Sandford Mead Pumping Station in 1905. Fresh water was pumped from the prolific spring here up to the Hewletts reservoirs.*

4 *Fossil ichthyosaur on display at the Cheltenham Ladies' College. A larger specimen was found in the clay near Malvern Road in 1899.*

The geology of the Cheltenham area has proved convenient for the supply of building materials. Bricks were probably first used in the town for chimneys in the timber-framed houses, but brick houses were built by wealthier residents from the 1600s. Cheltenham expanded rapidly during the 19th century, and the readily available Lias clay and local sand allowed enough bricks to be produced to build most of the original spa town. Relatively few buildings were faced with Cotswold limestone, the majority of terraces and villas being of stuccoed brick, and rows of artisan dwellings could be built cheaply using locally-made bricks. When the Colonnade was built off the High Street in 1791, there was sufficient clay on site to produce all the necessary bricks at 13s. per thousand. The *Plough Inn* was advertised for sale in 1795 with the advice that the kitchen garden and adjacent meadow would be suitable for making a large quantity of bricks. At the turn of the century there was a brickworks in Portland Street, and Mr Billings of Albion Cottage was letting a

brickworks with enough ground for three companies to work. In 1812 he advertised, in the *Cheltenham Chronicle*, the sale of a nine-acre Brick and Tile Manufactory in Coltham Field (near Haywards Road, possibly the site of the future Battledown Brickworks). Brick production was still largely localised, and the bricks for building St Margaret's Terrace in the 1820s are known to have been produced from the ground at the Hon. Miss Monson's nearby St Margaret's Villa. The burning brick clamps so near the centre of Cheltenham were a considerable nuisance factor.

As the 19th century progressed, brickmaking in Cheltenham removed to the outskirts of the new town and became more industrialised. In 1840 Frederick Thackwell started a brick, tile

5 *Calcutta Terrace, 163-9 St George's Road, built in the 1840s. The exposed brickwork of many of Cheltenham's artisan dwellings shows a chequered pattern of locally made bricks. (Photograph by Lisa Lavery.)*

and pottery works beside Leckhampton Road, including drainpipes, chimney pots and garden ware amongst his products. The six-acre Alstone Brick and Tile Works were for sale in 1855,

6　*Cheltenham College Chapel, opened in 1896. The interior contains much finely carved limestone.*

including a large dome-topped pottery kiln and three 61ft by 15ft drying sheds. John Williams & Co. bought the brickworks and modernised the brickmaking process by installing a steam pug mill for mixing the clay. Other brickworks appeared over the next 30 years, including James Leighton's Folly Lane brickworks, the Battledown Brick & Terra Cotta Co., founded by the Rev. Arthur Armitage in 1863, the Pilford Brickworks at Lower Pilley, begun in 1879, and William Smith's Atlas Brickworks, which was sold in 1882. In 1894 Roland and Harold Webb bought the Battledown Brick & Terra Cotta Co. and founded Webb Bros. The company subsequently bought out all the other Cheltenham brickmakers, and considerably expanded the business in the 20th century. One marketing ploy was its claim that brickmaking had first been established in Cheltenham by King Alfred the Great. The last visible reminder of brickmaking in Cheltenham, the 105ft chimney at the Battledown, was demolished in 1961, and the firm closed in 1971.

7　*The tower of Francis Close Hall, Swindon Road. Designed by Samuel Whitfield Daukes, this neo-Gothic building of 1849 is faced with local Ragstones.*

8　*Lake Cottage (now Pilgrim Cottage), Lake Street, Prestbury, photographed in 1906 following restoration. With 16th-century origins, the building is of brick, stone and timber, roofed with Cotswold stone tiles. Members of the Steel family were tenants of the cottage for 200 years.*

The other important building material available locally was Cotswold limestone, at one time intensively quarried on Leckhampton and Cleeve Hills. The Inferior Oolite freestone at Leckhampton has a fine-grained texture, almost devoid of large fossils, and can be freely sawn into blocks, making it useful for the classical architecture of Regency Cheltenham. Leckhampton stone was also used to build the Shire Hall in Gloucester, designed by Robert Smirke in 1816-18. Freestone weathers well if cut while the newly-extracted blocks are still moist and soft, and a protective coating forms as it dries out. The stone's fine texture also makes it ideal for delicate carving in interiors.

Hard limestones, known as Ragstones, which break into irregular lumps, top the freestone at Leckhampton. Ragstones were much used in dry stone walling, for metalling roads and in the later Neo-Gothic buildings such as Francis Close Hall (Swindon Road). There were many limekilns around the town during the spa building boom, where crushed limestone would be burned for use in lime mortar and putty. Limestone for Cheltenham was also quarried at Whittington (used to build Christ Church) and on Cleeve Hill, and in all these areas, including Leckhampton, the freestone was often extracted from mines tunnelled into the hillside. Rolling Bank Quarry on Cleeve Hill would regularly turn up large *Nautili*, up to 18 inches across, and Cheltenham inhabitants would roll these coiled fossils down the hill to their homes to use as garden ornaments and on rockeries.

Limestone was quarried at Leckhampton for centuries and was almost certainly used in the 12th century to build the parish church. John Norden's Survey of 1617 reported that at Leckhampton 'Mr Norwood takes the benefit of a moste large … quarry of excellent freestone'. In 1797 the Trye family officially re-opened the quarries, and the first-known goods railway in the county was installed shortly afterwards. This was a plate

9 *Hauling gravel in 1901 on Cleeve Hill. The Common was a much-exploited local source of materials for building and road mending.*

track, used to transport the large blocks of stone around the quarries. At about this time the Devil's Chimney, a column of rock jutting out from the face of the hill, had become a local landmark. Ruff wrote in his 1803 *History of Cheltenham*, 'Built by the devil, as say the vulgar. It was no doubt built by shepherds in the frolic of an idle hour'. It is thought more likely that the quarrymen had removed the surrounding stone *c.*1780 leaving the

10 *The Devil's Chimney, Leckhampton, from a drawing by Henry Lamb, c.1830. The cutting to the left of the chimney was made for the quarry tramroad, laid by Charles Brandon Trye of Leckhampton Court in the late 18th century.*

11 *Good Friday, 1902. A large crowd preparing to march up Leckhampton Hill in protest after the owner, Henry Dale, had closed footpaths and erected fences to prevent access. In 1929 the Council bought 3,000 acres of Leckhampton Hill for the people of Cheltenham.*

chimney, which would have made poor building stone, perhaps as a joke. In 1810 the horse-drawn Cheltenham & Leckhampton Tramway opened to transport the stone down to the town, following the line of Andover Road and Queens Road, which today lie diagonally across the grid pattern of later surrounding streets. Blocks of dressed stone costing 1d. per ton, including tramway delivery, were available from the stone wharves in Suffolk Road (later moved to Painswick Road), and at Alstone. Approximately 23,000 tons of stone were being carried annually along the tramway by 1838.

In 1897, after a century of ownership by the Trye family, John Henry Dale acquired the hill, forming the Leckhampton Quarries company two years later. By this time only the Leckhampton end of the tramway was still in use. There was outrage in 1902 when Dale attempted to close the hill to the public. For as long as anyone could remember the hill had been enjoyed for outings and public holidays, and the paths over

the hill formed the shortest route to town for the residents of Coberley and Cowley. Dale also owned a piano company and in response to his actions Dorothea Beale, headmistress of the Ladies' College, ordered him to remove all the pianos that the school had hired from his firm. A crowd gathered on the hill in March 1902, led by the 'Leckhampton Stalwarts', and destroyed the fences erected on it. Following the court appearance and acquittal of four 'Leckhampton Stalwarts', an even bigger crowd marched on the hill. They tore down Tramway Cottage, which had been erected on one of the favourite recreational spots, and further arrests were made. The battle continued over the next few years, culminating in the reading of the Riot Act on Good Friday 1906, and Dale eventually permitted the public to use the hill. After several attempts to keep the business going, including the introduction of blasting to extract the stone and the installation of four huge steel limekilns, the quarries finally closed in 1926.

There has only been a small amount of archaeological research within Cheltenham to tell us about the earliest settlers. A Neolithic long barrow or knap (4000-2000 B.C.) supposedly existed on part of the site of St James' Square, after which Knapp Lane was named. John Goding wrote, in his *History of Cheltenham* (1863), that this barrow was opened in 1832 to reveal three large upright stones and a capstone. The stone arrangement was left in situ as an object of interest until the railway arrived and the site was cleared in 1846. The capstone was used as a cider press at nearby Knapp House (demolished 1982). It would have been an unusual site for a long barrow, on low-lying land beside the river, and with no surviving evidence, modern techniques cannot be used to affirm that it was Neolithic. There have been chance finds of a few Neolithic stone axeheads and flint artefacts in Cheltenham, but little to suggest occupation of the area as early as this. A few sherds of Beaker pottery were discovered at Leckhampton, when a Bronze-Age site was being excavated at Sandy Lane, indicating possible late Neolithic activity in the area.

The excavations in Sandy Lane, carried out in 1951 and 1971, were to investigate a Bronze-Age burnt mound (2000-700 B.C.). The purpose of burnt mounds is still being debated, one possibility being to heat stones which were then dropped into a trough of water, either to provide steam for cooking or to heat the water making a type of 'slow-cooker' for meat. The important component of a boiling-pit was absent from the Sandy Lane site, possibly lying under modern housing beyond the excavation limits. The finds included a fragment of a clay mould for a late Bronze-Age spear, dating from *c.*1000 B.C., and it has been concluded that the burnt mound probably dates from this time.

There is little evidence of Iron-Age occupation (700 B.C.-A.D. 43), apart from a quantity of pottery at Sandy Lane. Some late Bronze-Age or Iron-Age

pottery has also been found at Rose Cottage in West Drive, Pittville. The presence of Iron-Age hill-forts on nearby Cleeve Hill, Crickley Hill and Leckhampton Hill suggests that indications of Iron-Age settlement and agricultural activity may yet be discovered in Cheltenham. Until recently it was thought that the Romans had largely ignored the site of Cheltenham as a place for settlement, as evidence of activity was limited to chance finds of Roman coins. However, during the last 30 years several areas have been identified which suggest Romano-British settlement. In 1979 a significant amount of Romano-British pottery was found in a trench at Coberley Road, Benhall, suggesting A.D. third-century occupation in this area. Romano-British

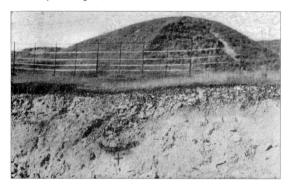

12 *Mid-Iron-Age remains (marked with a cross) revealed in 1903 in a gravel pit near King's Beeches on Cleeve Hill.*

13 *Archaeological dig at the St James' site, 2000-1, prior to the Waitrose development. Before traditional excavation methods could begin, up to six metres of ballast had to be stripped away using heavy machinery. Victorian engineers had dumped the ballast here to level the Chelt river valley before construction of the railway station in 1847.*

ditches have been found at Arle Court, and pottery dating from the first to the fourth centuries was excavated at Vineyards Farm, Charlton Kings along

14 *Archaeologist Sam Inder with an almost complete Severn Valley ware flagon, re-assembled from shards found during the St James' excavation. The pottery from the site dates from the second to mid-third centuries, and indicated that there was probably a substantial Roman settlement in the immediate vicinity.*

with fragments of wall-plaster. Recent excavations in the area of West Drive and Wellesley Road, Pittville have revealed ditches and trackways of a second- to fourth-century Romano-British field system, although the location of any associated settlement has not yet been identified. Evidence for Roman settlement has been found at Brizen Recreation Field, Up Hatherley Way, including part of a copper alloy brooch, a finger ring, fragments of stone walling, and two possible ditches or pits.

In 2003 the remains of a high-status Roman villa were discovered at Coberley, just outside Cheltenham. Part of a mosaic floor was uncovered, perhaps one of the largest ever found in the county. Limited excavation suggested that the mosaic consists of between nine and fifteen decorated panels, each about 1.4m sq., surrounded

by diamond pattern borders. Tesserae have been found in another part of the same field, suggesting a large villa or substantial farm. Other finds at the site included a quantity of Roman coins, pottery, parts of brooches, pins, thimbles and lead pot menders.

Nearer the centre of Cheltenham, excavations were carried out in the 1990's in the area behind St James' Square. A cold bath beside the River Chelt in this area, in use in the mid-18th century, was supposed to have Roman foundations, with the remains of a hypocaust under the floor, but no evidence remains. John Goding reported that a number of lead-lined coffins, thought to be Roman, were unearthed in the St James' area in the 19th century, but these finds were dispersed long ago and cannot be verified. The modern excavations uncovered two phases of a Romano-British ditched field system, a small number of pits and two graves, including one of an infant. The large quantity of pottery found during the excavations suggested that there was a substantial Roman settlement near the site, and established that there was considerable Roman settlement in the town during the second and third centuries.

No Saxon remains have been found to support brief documentary evidence of some sort of religious community at Cheltenham in the early ninth century, although there have been chance finds of Saxon iron spearheads. Much archaeology would have been lost during the expansion of the town in the 19th century, so even medieval and post-medieval finds have been few. We have to examine written records to unravel the early history of the Cheltenham we know today.

TWO

The Heyday of the Manor

The Saxons established Cheltenham at least 1,200 years ago, on the River Chelt beside the road from Winchcombe to Gloucester. At that time it was in the kingdom of Mercia, of which Winchcombe was once the capital. The name Cheltenham is thought to mean a settlement (ham) under a hill or cliff (chilt), appearing over the centuries as 'Chilteham', 'Chintenham' and 'Cheltham'. Leland, during his travels in the 1540s, referred to it as 'a long town having a market', calling it 'Cheltenham Street'. This layout reflects a typical Saxon origin of one long street with paths leading off into the fields on either side. A number of these narrow passages can still be seen leading off the High Street, some to the parish church.

The first known record of Cheltenham occurs in an account of the Council of Cloveshoe, held in A.D. 803, where a dispute was settled between the Bishops of Worcester and Hereford over which of them should receive the rents and profits of church lands at Cheltenham. It was stated that the Bishop of Worcester had drawn these revenues for the previous 30 years, suggesting that a small minster had been established at Cheltenham since at least A.D. 773. No further records of this early religious house have been found, and it was probably destroyed during the Danish invasions of the ninth century. It was traditionally located in the Cambray area, where a later grange belonging to Cirencester Abbey was sited, on land still belonging to the rectory of Cheltenham in the 17th and 18th centuries.

Cheltenham next appears in the Domesday Survey of 1086, having been in royal ownership since at least the time of Edward the Confessor. The Domesday entry describes not only the manor, but the royal hundred of Cheltenham, which included the outlying tithings and hamlets, approximately covering the area of the modern borough (excluding Prestbury, which was held by the Bishop of Hereford). From the brief information given, the population of Cheltenham has been estimated at 114 adult males. There were five mills along the Chelt between Charlton Kings and Arle, including two at Alstone and a forerunner to Barrett's Mill in Sandford Park. In King Edward's time 3,000 loaves were to be supplied annually for the dogs, suggesting a connection with royal hunting. This had been altered to a money tax by 1086. The church land was held by Reinbald,

15 *Arle Mill in the 1950s, one of the five mill sites mentioned in Domesday Book. (Photograph by G.M. Davis.)*

a wealthy Norman who was dean of a college of canons at Cirencester Abbey, to whom he left much of his property when he died. He was also the Chancellor of England for a time. Priests are mentioned at Cheltenham in Domesday Book, although the number is unspecified. A priory and a church with its chapels at Cheltenham are mentioned in a reference to a Gloucester Synod of 1086; the church was probably the predecessor of St Mary's parish church.

In 1133 Reinbald's property was transferred to the Augustinian Cirencester Abbey, which built St Mary's Church. The earliest parts of the church still extant are two external buttresses at the west end, and the pillars supporting the arches beneath the tower,

16 *North-east view of the parish church of St Mary, Cheltenham's only remaining medieval building. Most of the church dates from the 14th century, including the magnificent rose window.*

part of a church re-build in the late 12th century. These are virtually the only medieval remains to survive in Cheltenham. Cirencester Abbey held the church, supplying it with priests, until the Dissolution of the Monasteries in 1539, and it was during their ownership that the 14th-century Decorated-style windows were installed, including the magnificent circular rose window in the chantry dedicated to St Katherine. The cross in the churchyard also dates from this time.

St Mary's Church was the mother church to a number of chapels in the surrounding hamlets, including Arle providing a service three days a week in 1143, Leckhampton existing in 1162, and Charlton Kings dedicated *c.*1190. Another early

chapel held by the Cheltenham church was at Up Hatherley. There is a mention of a chapel in an entry for the tithing of Alstone in a Cheltenham Manor Court roll dated 4 May 1334: Richard Golde was fined for not maintaining the ditch between his holding and the Chapel of the Blessed Virgin Mary. This may, however, refer to the chapel at Arle, if his Alstone property was near the Arle boundary. In 1230 Robert Capellan had gifted land in Alstone to Llanthony Priory, and a Richard Capellan of Westal appears in a 1327 list of taxpayers. The word *capellano* means 'chaplain', and could be an occupational description, suggesting chapels at Alstone and at Westal. However, Capellan may have become a surname by this time.

17 *Leckhampton Court, 1820s, one of the oldest medieval manor houses in Gloucesteshire. This was the seat of the Norwood family for over 300 years, one of whom, William, was lord of the manor of Cheltenham from 1589-1616.*

18 *View towards the Lower High Street, 1804. The Market House of 1788 is centre right of the picture, and the entrance to the Colonnade, begun in 1791, is on the left.*

Being in royal possession the Manor of Cheltenham enjoyed many privileges, exempt from laws governing the rest of the country, and for this reason it was known as the 'Liberty of Cheltenham'. The tenants of the manor did not have to pay taxes to the Crown and were answerable to their own manor officials. In 1247 Henry III transferred the Liberty of Cheltenham, with attendant rights and privileges, and the Liberty of Slaughter to the Abbey of Fécamp, an order of monks from Normandy. The Liberties were exchanged for two strategic

20 *Mr Brookes of Uckington with two gleaners on his farm in 1915. Owing to the high price of wheat at the time, the old-fashioned practice of gleaning was temporarily restored.*

Channel ports, Rye and Winchelsea, which the King felt should no longer be in the hands of England's potential enemy. The Manor of Cheltenham remained in French monastic hands until 1414, when Henry V finally confiscated all their English lands. The King gave the manor to his Aunt, Elisabeth of Huntingdon, for her lifetime, before passing it to the Brigettine convent of Syon, a religious house he had founded at

Twickenham. So it remained until the Dissolution of the Monasteries by Henry VIII. It was not until the reign of Elizabeth I that Cheltenham had its first resident lord of the manor – William Norwood of Leckhampton.

Because Cheltenham was in royal and monastic possession, with absentee landlords, for so many centuries, it never had a castle or manor house to be developed into the focal great country house of a local squire. Mansions were built much later, but as residences for gentlemen in the new spa town. However, great families did establish fine homes on the outskirts of Cheltenham, such as the Greville family at Arle and the Norwoods at Leckhampton. In the centre of the town the only places of significance were the church, the market and the mills on the Chelt. There was also a courthouse, in which to conduct manorial business, situated approximately on the site of St Matthew's Church. A new Hall and Crosse Chamber were built in 1459, and in a Manor Court roll entry

19 *The wheat harvest at Leckhampton, 1901, a scene little changed in centuries.*

dated 17 August 1529 George Hurst was granted 'le court house' by the lady of the manor (the Abbess of Syon). This was on condition that the steward and justices could hold their courts during his lease without interference. He was still in possession at his death in 1541, and his widow and son continued with the remainder of the lease.

In 1226 Henry III granted Cheltenham the right to hold a market every Thursday and a three-day fair each July. Cheltenham was a suitable market location, being on the main route from Winchcombe to Gloucester. Competition arose when, in 1249, the Bishop of Hereford secured a market and fair for his Manor of Prestbury located on the same route. This situation was exceptional as market towns were usually established at approximate intervals of a day's cart movement. The addition of a market to its agricultural economy enabled Cheltenham to grow into a small town, with long narrow burgage plots added to the existing settlement either side of

21 'Cheltenham in the Olden Time', a somewhat fanciful view of early Cheltenham, published in 1857.

the main street. These were also approached from the rear by back lanes. The burgage plots were laid out from the High Street to the line of New Street, suggesting that the latter dates from at least this time. In the tax-list of 1307 Cheltenham appears as a recognised urban community, and as a borough in 1313. Burgage holders were exempted from agricultural services, being expected to make their living from trade and crafts. However, most continued to practise husbandry for their own benefit, and in Cheltenham they had sole right to use 20 acres of common in the Marsh to the north of the town (St Paul's area).

At this time the court held at Cheltenham was a hundred court, at which the bailiff of the borough made his presentments along with the men of the rural tithings. Over the centuries these tithings included Arle, Alstone, Ashley, Bafford, Bradwell (now part of Leckhampton), Charlton, Cheltenham (excluding the borough), Leckhampton, Naunton, Sandford, Swindon and Westal. A 'court baron' was usually held every three weeks at which fines and payments owed by tenants were collected, and complaints of debt or trespass were dealt with. A 'court leet' or 'view of frankpledge' could be held every six months or so, where cases of affray or

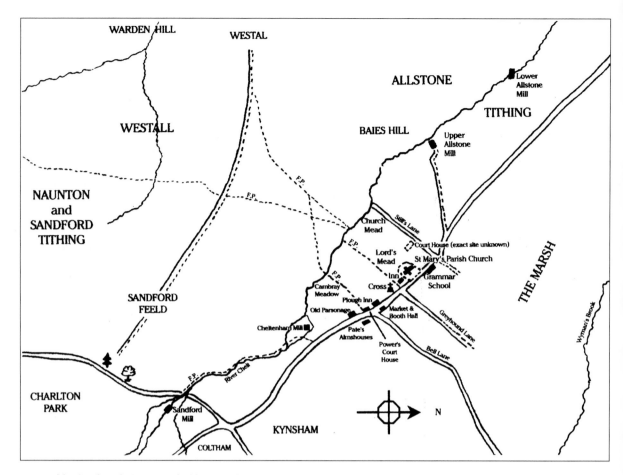

22 *Map based on the Report on the Manor of Cheltenham drawn up by topographer John Norden in 1617 on the order of James I, who wished to survey his Crown properties to ensure that full rents and profits were being paid. (Copied from a map prepared by Nancy Pringle and Gwen Hart, 1969.)*

common nuisance were presented. In Cheltenham these two types of court were often combined, usually presided over by a steward on behalf of the absentee landlord. In the early 16th century a purely manorial court was held, but by 1617 the borough had become independent, excluding the bailiff of the hundred-manor from a separate borough court.

The courts regulated the seasonal patterns of agriculture in the manor, ensuring the protection of crops. In Alstone tithing in June 1528 it was ordered that 'no beasts or sheep are to be pastured on the corn field called Sondfeld ..., on penalty of a fine

23 *Tudor Cottage, 1928. Formerly known as the Old Farm, this ancient timbered house was situated on Gloucester Road between the Primary School and the Tesco site. At a cost of £500 it was carefully removed from here in 1929, to be re-erected at the entrance to Rossley Manor opposite Dowdeswell Reservoir.*

24 The High Street and the Plough, c.1740, when most of the buildings in Cheltenham were still timbered and thatched. The River Chelt was regularly diverted along the centre of the street to clean the highway, hence the stepping-stones.

of 6s 8d'. In the same court roll the tenants of Bafford tithing were ordered that 'all pigs be kept ringed' between August and February, presumably to manure the land without uprooting the crops. The agricultural system involved a number of large open fields around the town, divided into strips, which were allocated to the tenants for cultivation. This type of field layout also occurred in the surrounding hamlets. Some of Cheltenham's streets, such as St Paul's Lane and Lypiatt Street, still retain a reverse 'S' shape, reflecting the pattern of ridge-and-furrow ploughing whereby the team of oxen turned the plough at each headland. Old field names are echoed in modern street names, such as Northfield Passage and Kingsmead Avenue.

At the manor courts each tithing regularly presented a common fine in lieu of services to the lord. Other methods of raising revenue included the setting of assizes (standards of weight, measure and quality), which were regularly broken by the tradesmen, who were then fined. This could be considered a form of business rate, and those fined included bakers, brewers, butchers, millers, shoemakers and tanners. One name that occurred frequently in the court rolls of the 1520s was Walter Pate, father of Richard Pate who founded the Grammar School. Walter broke the assize as a butcher, baker and … chandler. He also kept an inn and, with Thomas Lynet, held a water mill at Westal. In December 1528 Walter was fined for breaking into the mill at Sandford, in which he also had a share, and damaging Thomas Lynet's property. The court records show that, besides the water mills on the River Chelt and Hatherley Brook, horse-operated grain mills were in use at this time.

Crimes were dealt with by the manor court, with men from the tithing called as witnesses to decide an offender's guilt. In an entry for Charlton dated 9 October 1528 the tithing was ordered to make a pair of stocks to punish felons, transgressors and disturbers of the peace. The

25   Fire at Redgrove Cottage, Hesters Way, 1929. The thatched and timbered cottage was rapidly gutted by the fire.

whole tithing would be held liable for failure to maintain roads, bridges and ditches, or for allowing poaching in the lord's warren and fishponds. In the same court roll it was recorded that every inhabitant of Westal must 'repair his own part of the highway between Westhall Grene and the stone bridge, and the bridge itself, so that the King's subjects can cross safely'. Individual cases of nuisance were many and varied. On 8 August 1527 Elena Barks was fined as a common eavesdropper, and William Foster assaulted William Ermyt with a bill hook. On 28 November 1527 Thomas Church was ordered to remove his dung heap from the king's highway in Colamstrete (in Leckhampton), while Giles Westby and George Goderich, of Charlton, and Henry Nedeham, a chaplain of Shipton Solers, were charged with corrupting an 18-year-old named William. They enticed him to gamble at cards and dice, causing him to sell his tunic: 'Giles and George took his money and sent him away naked in his shirt and hose.'

Medieval justice was often harsh by today's standards and women's rights were few. In 1330 Alice, the wife of Henry of Upatherle (Up Hatherley), presented a plea to the king, Edward I. Her husband had been imprisoned by the Scots at the Battle of Stirling, and released over a year later having paid a ransom of £40. During his absence Thomas of Upatherle and Robert of Prestbury had taken over Henry's fields at Upatherle, demolishing his houses and taking his belongings. On Henry's return from his ordeal in Scotland they 'raised the hue and cry' against him, claiming that he, Henry, had robbed Thomas of goods worth £100. Their story was believed and Henry was imprisoned in Gloucester Castle, awaiting the arrival of the justices. When he was eventually set free he obtained a writ against Thomas and Robert. However, the two villains came to meet him in Gloucester where they attacked him 'and quite wrecked and vilely treated his body, so that he barely escaped death'. The King's response to Alice's plea was hardly satisfactory: 'If the husband be alive, the plaint is his; if he be dead, the wife's plaint is nothing.'

The rights of women were to improve in the 17th century following the Cheltenham Act of 1625. Much of the land in Cheltenham was copyhold land belonging to the manor. This property could only be transferred through the manor courts, whether by sale or inheritance, with payment of fines and heriots to the lord each time it changed hands. The copy of the transaction in the court rolls proved the tenants' title to the property. In the Middle Ages the lord of the manor could claim a copyholder's 'best beast' on his death. The Act of 1625 clarified the rights of the tenants and their obligations to the lord of the manor, and also changed the system of inheritance.

26 Lower Alstone House. Built c.1700 as a residence for Richard Hyett, Gentleman, this house suffered a gradual loss of status when it became the home of a potato merchant and then of a fellmonger in the 19th century. Following the removal of the neighbouring skinyard, the house has recently been restored. (Photograph by Lisa Lavery.)

Borough English, whereby the youngest son was considered the legal heir, had been the norm prior to this. The Act established that a widow was entitled to 'freebench' of one third of her husband's copyhold land, unless she had agreed to the sale of any of it during his lifetime. This right was dramatised in an extended court case during the 1830s involving the widow of Col Riddell. The Colonel arrived in Cheltenham c.1800, already separated from his wife, and lived as a bachelor there until his death in 1825. During that time he bought and sold considerable amounts of property around the town. His widow seemed unaware of his death or any entitlement until 1830 when she started legal proceedings to recover her widow's freebench. In 1835 the courts had found in her favour, and Mrs Riddell proceeded to enter many of the Colonel's former properties in pursuance of her claims. Included amongst these properties was 8 St George's Place (now 22), which Col Riddell had sold with the garden land opposite to Dr Edward Jenner in November 1804.

Cheltenham was touched by war on two occasions, the first time with little effect. On 3 May 1471 Edward IV passed through the town on the eve of the Battle of Tewkesbury, with an army consisting of 3,000 infantry and a large body of cavalry. He stayed for some refreshment and caused his army to 'do the like'. Although this would have presented a tremendous burden to the town, there was apparently no blood shed. During the Civil War Cheltenham was more closely involved, mainly on the Royalist side, as John Dutton, the lord of the manor, was a supporter of the King. On 14 February 1643 Charles I wrote from Oxford to the Steward of the Manor, John Stubbes in Charlton Kings, asking for a loan of £20, 'or the value thereof in plate'. While Charles I was laying siege to the city of Gloucester, the Parliamentarian Earl of Essex spent the night of 4 September 1643 with his forces on Cleeve Hill. The next day they marched to Cheltenham where they overcame some resistance before spending the next three days resting in the town. Charles abandoned his siege on hearing the guns of Essex's army, leaving the city in the hands of Col Massey. In November Massey planned an attack on Cheltenham to seize the rents due to be paid to John Dutton by the tenants. Lord Chandos rode from Sudeley with 100 foot and 120 horse and saved Cheltenham from the raiders, despite being attacked at Prestbury on his way home. In 1863 John Goding wrote, in his *History of Cheltenham*, of a considerable number of bodies being found in the area of St James' Square, along with soldiers' buttons and other relics of the Civil War.

On the eve of the discovery of the mineral waters Cheltenham was still a relatively small market town, described by John Prinn, Steward of the Manor, as having 321 houses with 1,500

27 The last Court Leet, held on 13 November 1925. Posing for the photograph are the Steward, Constables, Jurymen, Tithingmen and the Crier.

inhabitants in the parish. The single main street was lined with gabled thatched cottages, behind many of which would have been malthouses. Despite brick chimneys, the risk of fire was great, and Cheltenham suffered a disastrous fire in the summer of 1719. It was severe enough to be mentioned in church briefs around the country well into the following year. For example, in December 1719 the congregation at Croxhall church, Lichfield, gave their collection to the 'poor sufferers by fire at Cheltenham'. Paving was limited to the sides of the street, and there were few high-status houses in the town. Sir Robert Atkyns, in his *History of Gloucestershire* (1712), wrote that Mr Mitchell had a good house and estate. This was the property known as Powers Court, sited on the corner of Rodney Road. Atkyns also wrote that Mr Hiet had a good house and estate at Alstone. This was Lower Alstone House, built *c.*1703, which survives as Cheltenham's only Queen Anne house.

The Manor of Cheltenham finally ceased being in royal possession in 1628, shortly after the passing of the Cheltenham Act, and was sold to John Dutton of Sherborne for £1,200. It remained with this family for the next 200 years, during which time the town yet again had an absentee landlord.

In 1843 Lord Sherborne sold the manor to James Agg-Gardner, a successful brewer in the town, for £39,000. The new lord's steward increased the manorial fees, which had remained virtually unchanged for centuries, but the copyholders won a court case in 1853 resisting these increases. In 1862 Robert Sole Lingwood, solicitor, bought the manor as a business speculation. He pressed the copyholders to enfranchise their property (that is, convert it to freehold) at their great cost, and advised them that he would be claiming for any timber felled, or clay dug for brickmaking, on copyhold property without permission of the lord of the manor. A four-day inquiry into these claims was held in 1863, at which the copyholders' solicitor quoted from the Domesday entry and the Cheltenham Act of 1625 as evidence against Lingwood's proposals. Elderly copyholders witnessed that they had never paid any forfeit for timber and clay since the days of Lord Sherborne. The copyholders won their case, and the Manor of Cheltenham continued to collect only nominal rents and fines until copyhold tenure was finally abolished in an Act of 1925. Thus the last remnants of the powerful medieval manorial system disappeared.

THREE

Discovery and Development

Although Camden, who compiled the first topographical survey of England (1586), had commented on the medicinal qualities of Cheltenham's springs, the town seems to have ignored its local waters until the 18th century. In 1704 William Mason, a hosier and Quaker, bought Bayshill field in Alstone Tithing from Mr Higgs of Charlton Kings. A mineral spring was found in the field in 1716 (now under the site of the Princess Hall, Cheltenham Ladies' College), a 'discovery' traditionally attributed to pigeons pecking at the surrounding salts. However, another story ascribes the discovery to the miraculous recovery of a sick horse after drinking from the spring. In 1718, having purchased the adjoining land, Mr Mason sank a well to collect the mineral water, and built a rustic Well House. By 1720 advertisements had appeared for the famous purging Cheltenham waters, with the added attraction of a fine bowling green nearby. The following year Doctors Greville and Baird undertook the first analysis of the saline water, confirming it to be a mild chalybeate. In the late 1720s the novelist Daniel Defoe predicted, 'The mineral waters lately discovered … are what will make this place more and more remarkable and frequented.'

The mineral spring was leased to a Mr Spencer until the later 1730s, during which time the waters were first bottled and sold outside the town. In 1738 William Mason's son-in-law, a Manx sea captain named Henry Skillicorne, retired from Bristol to Cheltenham and developed the site of the original spring. Skillicorne planted the Well Walk avenue of trees, deepened the original well, laid out a paved court and replaced the wooden shelter with a more substantial arched brick canopy. West of the well he erected the large 'Old Room' with a billiard room above, providing subscribers with further shelter and the opportunity for dancing. He completed the development with 18 small 'necessary houses' ('necessary' because of the rapid loosening effects of the waters), which were removed in the 1820s to make way for Montpellier Street. Lodgings were scarce at this time with only two inns, the *Plough* and the *George*, providing accommodation. In 1739 the widowed Lady Stapleton built Grove House, or the Great House (site of St Matthew's Church), which provided lodgings later in the century, by which time the *Crown*, the *Swan* and the *Fleece* accommodated visitors.

The timely publication of Dr Short's favourable analysis of the spa water in 1740 provided a boost to Skillicorne's enterprise, and in 1743 there were 667 subscribers to the well, including many peers of the realm. At this time the Cheltenham waters could be bought for 9d. per sealed bottle outside the county. In the 1750s Thomas Hughes, an attorney from Monmouthshire, became keeper of the well. He developed the manufacture and sale of Cheltenham waters and mineral salts, which were packed in bottles in the Old Room. Agents were appointed around the country and

28 *A pigeon tops a gatepost at The Crippetts, Leckhampton. These gates once stood at one of the entrances to the Original Well. Credited with discovering the mineral spring, pigeons feature on the borough coat of arms and on tourist signposts. Appropriately, the Royal Pigeon Racing Association has its headquarters at The Reddings. (Photograph by Lisa Lavery.)*

by 1752 the mineral water was being exported from Bristol. In partnership with John de la Bere, Hughes prospered as a lawyer, moving his interests to the upper High Street area, where he established entertainments to rival those at the Old Well. Amongst other property, he bought the old Powers Court estate next to the *Plough*, which included a ballroom and gardens run by Mrs Jones. He also built several fine lodging-houses in the Upper High Street, and the 'Keynsham' street names off the London Road, which assimilate an earlier field-name of 'Kingsham', may have been named after his wife, Elizabeth Bridges, the joint heiress of Keynsham, North Somerset.

Henry Skillicorne died in 1763 and his memorial tablet in the parish church, chronicling

his life, is the longest in Britain. His son, Capt. William Skillicorne, took over the Bayshill property, replacing Hughes with William Miller as tenant of the well. In 1772 Hannah Forty was appointed Pumper at the Old Wells, holding the post for 43 years until shortly before her death in 1816. William Skillicorne built Cheltenham's first Long Room and converted the Old Room into private dwellings. In 1784 Thomas Hughes opened the Lower Assembly Rooms in the High Street, replacing these with larger Assembly Rooms in 1810. In competition William Miller opened the Upper Assembly Rooms further up the High Street in 1791, but they were not a commercial success and had become R. Crump's Universal Auction Room by 1809. Another diversion for visitors was to ride out to Gallipot Farm to drink syllabubs under the trees. The Earl of Suffolk built Suffolk House there in the early 1800s, leading to the development of Suffolk Square in the 1820s. As the number of visitors increased towards the end of the century, it was felt necessary to elect Cheltenham's first Master of the Ceremonies, Simeon Moreau of Bath. Appointed in 1786, it was during his reign that Cheltenham's future as a spa became assured.

In July 1788 George III, accompanied by Queen Charlotte and three royal princesses, arrived for a five-week visit, to take the waters on the advice of Sir George Baker, president of the Royal College of Physicians. The royal visitors stayed at Fauconberg Lodge, Bayshill, to which 17 rooms had to be added to accommodate them. The quarters were still cramped, especially when the King's son, the Duke of York, joined the party. The *Gentleman's Magazine* reported that, having spotted a neatly built timber house complete with sash windows at the end of the town, the King suggested it might be transported to the royal lodgings. Mr Ashton, an ingenious mechanic and surveyor, organised this removal despite having to

29 Old Well Walk looking south, c.1826. Henry Skillicorne developed the original spring from 1738. Assisted in the design by Norborne Berkeley, Skillicorne laid out the 900-yard avenue of elms. Planted by local surveyor Paul Andrews, it provided a vista down the slopes of Bayshill towards the parish church.

negotiate a small bridge, and a climb of 50 feet. It took 20 or 30 men six days, much longer than the King had expected, and he prevented them from erecting it on the bowling green where it would have spoiled his servants' play. The wooden house remained on the spot for several years after the royal visit.

The King paid daily early morning visits to the Old Well, but the volume of mineral water was proving to be insufficient. Fortunately a new saline well was accidentally discovered whilst digging for a fresh water supply for Fauconberg Lodge. Named the King's Well, or Royal Spa, it was sited in what is now Overton Road; it had closed by 1809. The King spent his days walking around the town and on scenic tours of the area, including visits to local farms. On two occasions he visited

John Boles Watson's theatre, which had been built in York Passage in 1782, where he saw the actress Mrs Jordan. His attendance earned both the theatre and the Old Well the right to add 'Royal' to their names. His presence attracted enormous attention to the town and the *Morning Post* reported, 'The Cheltenham cap – the Cheltenham bonnet – the Cheltenham buttons – the Cheltenham buckles – all the fashions are completely Cheltenhamised.' Following the departure of the royal visitors, the Master of the Ceremonies, Simeon Moreau, commissioned a commemorative medal in honour of their visit, and copies were presented to the royal family the following year.

Expansion of Cheltenham was gradual following the royal visit, gaining momentum after 1800. In 1788-9 development started in St George's

30 *The royal visitors taking an airing outside Fauconberg Lodge in 1788. William Skillicorne was commissioned to build the house on Bayshill by Henry, 3rd Earl of Fauconberg, who visited the town in 1776 hoping to cure a facial sore.*

31 *The Old Farm, St George's Place, c.1860. This was the home of the Skillicorne family from 1738 when Henry Skillicorne retired from Bristol to develop the spa in Cheltenham. It was demolished c.1869 to make way for the Shaftesbury Hall (now part of Chelsea Square).*

32 *Regency ironwork at Pittville Lawn, based on a design by architect Henry Shaw that was first published in 1826. These buildings were completed by 1834. (Photograph by David Kemish.)*

Place, then known as Still's Lane. The Skillicorne family lived here at the Old Farm, on the main route to the Royal Well and Fauconberg Lodge. Mr Lambert, owner of a livery stables in St George's Place, built the first row of houses in the lane, one of which was bought by Dr Jenner as his residence in 1804. Jenner wrote to a friend in 1805, 'So great has been the scramble for Houses in this favourite haunt of the great and opulent, that I have been obliged to be a buyer in order to secure a place to hide my little Head in.'

These early brick-built, stuccoed houses, with their ornamental ironwork, set the pattern for the Regency Cheltenham. In 1826, when the style had become firmly established, Fosbroke commented that 'the houses, verandas, and iron rails, look as if

they were composed of paper, silk, and netting'. In 1791 the Colonnade was built, a block of houses and shops, leading out of the High Street. The opening created by the Colonnade led towards the future Promenade, developed largely by the Harward family and Thomas Henney 30 years later. Over the next half-century Cheltenham developed as a series of estates centred around spas, this growth becoming feasible with the 1801 Enclosure Act, which released land for building from the shared open-field system.

As the reputation of the spa grew, it became necessary to find other sources of mineral water. For many years the local inhabitants had been drinking the water from a chalybeate spring near the banks of the River Chelt, reputed to cure

33 The Promenade, photographed by a visitor, E.C.S. Cole, 1883. The Promenade was laid out in 1818, across former brickfields, as a tree-lined ride towards the Sherborne Spa (later the Queen's Hotel *site). Development of a hotel, villas and terraces followed in 1823.*

34 *The Cambray or Chalybeate Spa opened in Rodney Road, 1834. It was converted into a Turkish bath by William Ruck in 1873 and demolished in 1938.*

weakness and diseases of the eyes. In 1801 William Humphrey Barrett exploited this local knowledge, laying out gravelled paths and erecting a large room over the spring. The cure of Sir Francis Burdett, a renowned politician, established the spring's reputation, but this original chalybeate well had become a private house by the 1850s. A part of it still survives in the corner of Sandford Park beside College Road.

In 1807 another chalybeate well was established at Fowler's Cottage (in Rodney Road), and a new, octagonal Cambray Spa replaced this in 1834. Older residents remember this building as the Turkish Baths, before demolition in 1938. Development of Cambray mushroomed with the discovery of the chalybeate springs. The chief entrepreneurs were John Boles Watson, who built a new Theatre Royal, Baynham Jones, who built Cambray House, and Col John Riddell. Watson sold some land to

Col Riddell, hoping he would not object to the strange-tasting water from the pump there. Riddell suspected it might be medicinal mineral water and, following his purchase, property prices in the area doubled. Riddell built a large house on the future Bath Road, called Wellington Mansion in honour

35 *Montpellier Spa, 1840s. The colonnade was designed in 1817 by G.A. Underwood, who had been an assistant to Sir John Soane. Behind this is the domed rotunda, added in 1825 to the designs of John Buonarotti Papworth.*

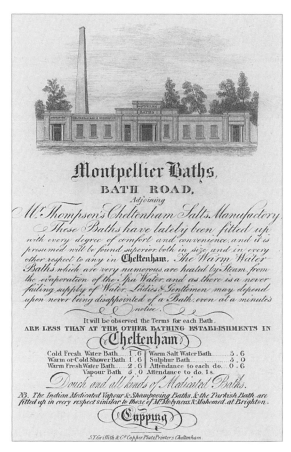

36 *Advertisement for the Montpellier Baths and Salts Manufactory, 1826. The building remained in use for bathing into the 20th century. It was converted into a public swimming pool by the Borough Council in 1898 and a new suite of Medical Baths was opened in 1919. In April 1945 the baths were converted into the Civic Playhouse.*

37 *The rustic Pumper's Cottage, with a tank housed in the adjacent wooden tower. Spa water was collected here from Thompson's numerous wells in Lansdown and Montpellier, before being pumped down to the Salts Manufactory over a mile away in Bath Road. This cottage remained beside Christ Church Road until late in the 19th century.*

of the Duke of Wellington who stayed there on two occasions.

A major developer who was responsible for the expansion of Cheltenham was a Liverpool and London banker, Henry Thompson, who in 1801 bought the 400 acres of land on which Montpellier and Lansdown now stand. In 1804 he built Hygeia House, now Vittoria House, as his first spa. Over the next few years Thompson laid out the walks and rides of Montpellier, reflected in the Montpellier road pattern today. In March 1808 he opened the first Montpellier Well, erecting a wooden pump-room and long-room over it the following year. G.A. Underwood rebuilt this, adding a plain Doric colonnade in 1817. Thompson also installed mineral water pumps in a small Octagon Turret by Gothic Cottage in Montpellier Field.

To counteract the shortage of mineral water Henry Thompson promoted bathing as an alternative to drinking the waters. This idea was not new to Cheltenham: in 1763 a Miss Stapleton had kept a cold bath, with facilities for warm bathing, beside the River Chelt near the present St James' Square. It was disused by 1783, but four years later Mr Freeman opened a suite of warm and tepid Medicinal Baths at 61 High Street. Henry Thompson opened his Montpellier Baths in the new Bath Road, offering 14 warm baths and one large cold bath. The benefits of bathing, as a supplement to drinking the waters, were confirmed by Dr Thomas Jameson in his *Treatise on the Cheltenham Waters*, and Thompson's Baths received over 100 visitors a week in 1809. Other bathing establishments existed in Cheltenham over the years, including the outdoor Parker's Swimming and Bathing Place in the 1820s, sited at the west end of the present *Exmouth Arms* garden. During the 1830s Thornton's Baths in Tavistock Place (Rodney Road) were particularly recommended for skin disorders, and the Cheltenham Hydropathic Institution, at the corner of Sherborne Place and Fairview Road, offered cold water cures from 1842-64.

Henry Thompson established a Salts Manufactory as part of the Montpellier Baths. Cheltenham Salts were being produced at the Old Well by Paytherus & Co., marketed by Savory, Moore & Co., until business slumped in 1815. Thompson worked on a grander scale, sinking over 70 wells in Montpellier and Lansdown, from which

38 *Advertisement for Chelspa, c.1930, produced by the United Chemists' Association Ltd (UCAL) which was established at Priory Court in 1915. By June that first year the demand for the waters all over Britain exceeded supply. The firm expanded in Corpus Street producing lozenges, tablets and liquid remedies. It closed in 1972.*

several thousand feet of lead pipes took the spa water to the Salts Manufactory. Thompson's salts were sold in Bath, London, Dublin and Edinburgh, but the business suffered a setback when rumours arose about their composition. It was suggested that a certain black wagon journeyed weekly to and from Epsom, possibly supplying some powerful ingredient for the preparation of the salts. A few years later, in 1820, Dr Adam Neale published a letter that cast doubt on the genuineness of the Cheltenham waters. Although this was immediately refuted in a letter from Dr Jameson, it was found that Epsom salts had been thrown daily into one of the wells, although not one of Thompson's. Over the next half-century Cheltenham never quite lost its reputation for offering adulterated waters, but by then it did not matter; the town had become well-known for its retirement prospects and educational provision, and its future lay in its residents rather than its visitors.

In 1824 Pearson Thompson inherited his father's land and business interests, and immediately set about developing Montpellier and Lansdown. His architect, John Buonarotti Papworth, erected a domed rotunda over the Montpellier Spa and designed the sumptuous interior, including the pump fixtures and fittings. Behind the stone lion above the entrance, and, curiously, out of sight from the ground, is the carved motto 'Infirmo capiti fluit utilis utilis alvo', which roughly translates as 'Our waters cure head and stomach aches'. At this time the Cheltenham waters were recommended for, among other disorders, indigestion, hypochondriasis, bilious complaints, visceral obstructions, obstinately costive habits, feminine complaints, consumption, scrofula, tumours and worms.

Papworth, whose Cheltenham buildings included St John's Church, Berkeley Street (now demolished), also designed the layout of the Lansdown estate, described by David Verey as

39 *Lansdown Crescent, c.1928. Although J.B. Papworth was responsible for the semi-circular layout, R.W. and C. Jearrad were the architects who completed the buildings by 1838. The enclosed gardens and tennis courts to the left of the photograph are now an open green space for all to enjoy.*

'the first English garden city'. The development was continued by R.W. and C. Jearrad, successful developer-architects comparable with Burton and Cubitt. They dismissed Papworth in 1830, refusing to pay him and retaining his plans against his wishes. Charles Jearrad worked from their London practice, but his brother, Robert William, moved to Cheltenham and was able to oversee the building of the Crescent, terraces and Italianate villas of the Lansdown estate. Ironically, he himself lived with his family in an ancient timbered farmhouse at Westal Green. Other buildings by Jearrad include the *Queen's Hotel* (1838), the Gothic Christ Church (1840) and Christ Church School, Malvern

Road (1850). He also designed the rebuilding of Boddington Manor, a few miles from Cheltenham, in Gothic Revival style. Thompson continued his development of Montpellier, laying out Montpellier Gardens to Papworth's designs. South of the Rotunda a row of private lodging houses called Ormond Villas was built in 1825-6. They were converted to shops by 1844, after development along the formerly tree-lined Montpellier Walk had begun. W.H. Knight designed the shops there in classical style, punctuated by a series of white statues, the caryatids.

Despite the Thompsons' enterprise at Montpellier, there was still a shortage of mineral

40 *The white statues between the shops in Montpellier Walk are caryatids, armless Grecian virgins copied from the Erectheum at Athens. The first three were sculpted in terracotta by Rossi, and the rest copied in stone by James Brown of Tivoli, later of Malvern Road. (Photograph by David Kemish.)*

water and a demand for building land. Between 1801 and 1821 the population rose from 3,076 to 13,388, and although 1,700 new houses had been built in that time, the number of visitors was also increasing. The discovery of saline water north of the town prompted another developer, Joseph Pitt, to lay out the Pittville estate in the 1820s on land he had acquired beside the Prestbury Road. Joseph Pitt was a successful solicitor with land interests in Cheltenham and in Wiltshire, where he became MP for Cricklade in 1812. Pitt had already developed land in Cheltenham with the building of the town's first terrace, Royal Crescent, from 1805, and he had completed many of the houses of Cambray Place by 1817.

The architect John Forbes designed the Pump Room and the layout of the estate for Joseph Pitt, and a local nurseryman, Richard Ware, landscaped the grounds in 1827. Pittville Pump Room is a classically-inspired two-storey building, topped by a dome and surrounded on three sides by a colonnade of Ionic columns. The foundation stone was laid on 4 May 1825, and the building took five years to complete. Unfortunately Forbes' career ended in disgrace when he was imprisoned for forging an employer's name on bills of exchange. From 1836 Henry Merrett was employed as the estate architect, ensuring that the many individual builders conformed to the overall plan and style. Joseph Pitt had envisaged a 100-acre estate containing 500 houses, with tree-lined walks and rides crossing park-like surroundings, but by 1860 less than half of these houses had been built. Pitt's scheme, which included Clarence and Wellington Squares, was only a partial success; the attractions south of the High Street continued to rival Pittville, and a slump in the building boom in 1826 delayed progress, severely limiting the hoped-for financial returns.

Other spas were opened around the town, but they never achieved the popularity and fashionable status of Montpellier and Pittville. Lord Sherborne's well was established in 1804 on the site of the present Gordon Lamp, to be succeeded in 1816 by the Sherborne or Imperial Spa at the top of the Promenade. To make way for the building of the *Queen's Hotel* in 1838, this spa building was moved further down the Promenade to the corner of St George's Road, and survived another 100 years before being demolished. In 1809 Mr Smith discovered a mineral spring in the grounds of his Alstone Villa, near Upper Alstone Mill. He erected an octagonal pump room there, surrounded by Jung and Schneider's Nursery Gardens. Alstone Spa closed in 1834, although it did enjoy a brief revival in the early 1900s, when

41 *Pittville Pump Room, 1820s, drawn by its architect John Forbes. Following disagreements between Forbes and the builder, a second architect, John Clement Mead, was employed to finish the interior.*

the waters were dispensed from a timbered shelter opposite the Corporation Swimming Baths.

In 1837 a mineral spring was discovered in the Park area but was not exploited until 1850, by which time the fashion for spas was fading. Development had already begun in the area in 1833-4, when Thomas Billings laid out the short-lived Gloucestershire Zoological, Botanical and Horticultural Gardens. The subsequent owner,

42 *Alstone Spa, Great Western Road, 1903. The site was cleared to make way for the recent development of the St James' area.*

architect Samuel Whitfield Daukes, built several of the villas around the perimeter. Several other wells were opened in the Lansdown and Christchurch areas in the second half of the 19th century. Chadnor Villa Well, in Well Place, and Lansdown Terrace Well were opened in 1857, and as late as 1885 the Fulshaw Lodge Well in Christ Church Road was established. These were short-lived, however, and in 1906 the Borough Council started a new drive to promote Cheltenham as a spa. A new Central Spa was opened in the recently built Town Hall, where women in frilled aprons and caps dispensed the waters of the Montpellier and Pittville Spas. By the end of the 20th century the only pump remaining in public use was at Pittville Pump Room. In 2003 even this supply failed when it was found that the original well shaft had cracked, allowing groundwater to dilute the spa. The days when people believed in the healing properties of spa water had long gone, but an appeal was immediately launched to fund a new bore hole to re-establish the original supply; Cheltenham Spa without spa water would be unthinkable.

43 *The Duke of Wellington regularly drank the waters during his visits, and was always accompanied by large crowds eager to catch a glimpse of the hero of Waterloo.*

FOUR

Acquiring a Reputation

From the late 18th century military officers and civilian officials of the East India Company began to flock to Cheltenham to retire. The mild saline waters were particularly recommended as a palliative for tropical disease and conditions of the liver and digestion, and the sheltered location made the town especially attractive to those who had spent many years in Bombay, Madras or Bengal, or at other East India Company posts. Cheltenham was said to have a climate much like Simla, the hill station in north-eastern India which served as the summer capital for the British. The Duke of Wellington took the waters in 1805 as a health cure following service in India, and visited on three further occasions, including 1816 following his triumphant victory over Napoleon at Waterloo. Wellington is said to have recommended the waters to fellow soldiers, which probably encouraged many to settle in the town. Between 1712 and the 1801 census, Cheltenham's population doubled to over 3,000; by 1826 the population of the town had grown to 20,000, and by 1851 to 35,000. With the increasing number of residents came a need for suitable housing. Military personnel occupied many of the newly built properties, particularly in Pittville and Lansdown.

Charles Sturt, Military Secretary to Ralph Darling, Governor of New South Wales, retired to Cheltenham in 1853, dying there in 1869. Darling was already living in retirement at Lansdown Terrace, which possibly influenced Sturt's move.

Between 1828-44 Sturt, a born leader, enthusiastic botanist, and talented writer and artist, had led a number of expeditions into the unexplored interior of Australia, where he is still remembered for his courage and endurance; an Australian wild flower, Sturt's Desert Pea, was named after him. Lieut-Col William Nicol Burns and his brother Col James Glencairn Burns, sons of the Scottish national poet Robert Burns, both retired to Cheltenham after serving with the East India Company. They lived at Glencairn, a large house facing Lansdown Road, on a site now occupied by Glencairn Park Road.

There are many memorials in the town to those with military and colonial connections, including a memorial in Christ Church, to Lieut-Col Kennedy, founder of Simla. Most of the 181 tablets in Holy Trinity Church are to Officers and Indian Civil Servants, including one to Lieut-Col Boden, founder of a Sanskrit professorship at Oxford. W.E. Adams, recalling his childhood in Cheltenham *c.*1840, wrote that 'you couldn't fire a shot-gun in any direction without hitting a Colonel'. Following the Indian Mutiny in 1857, local newspapers reported that hundreds of Cheltenham families were waiting anxiously for news of friends or relations. Many Old Cheltonians fought in the Mutiny, and Cheltenham College's first chapel had more tablets to those who died in the Mutiny than to those who fell in the Crimea. Cheltenham became known as the Anglo-Indian

44 *The Anglo-Indian entrance screen to the market, as drawn by Edward Jenkins who was probably the architect. The screen included the centre stone from which distances to other towns and cities were measured.*

town, retaining its 'retired colonels' image well into the 20th century.

With such strong connections it is perhaps surprising that there are so few echoes of India in Cheltenham's architecture. Two houses in Bath Road, Malcolm Ghur and Mosquito Ghur, listed by 1830, suggest an Anglo-Indian connection, Ghur being Hindi for house. An area of town at the junction of Gloucester Road and St George's Road became known as Calcutta, centred round the *Calcutta Inn*, first listed in 1841. However, despite their names, all these buildings were of English appearance. In fact the retired military men and civil servants would have felt very much at home in Cheltenham, as under British rule many of the new buildings in India were neo-classical or Grecian in style. The only significant, direct

architectural reference to India in Cheltenham was the entrance screen of the Market Arcade on the High Street, completed in 1823. Probably designed by local architect Edward Jenkins, it had three arches with peacock-tail heads, and dividing pillars, pinnacles and battlements. This distinctive landmark, with the arcade and market that lay behind it, was demolished following the market's closure in 1867.

The Evangelical Revival, spread throughout India by Bishop Heber and his missionaries, also had a profound influence in Cheltenham. The ex-colonial residents would have appreciated this, particularly following the appointment of Francis Close, initially as curate-in-charge of the newly built Holy Trinity in 1824. Close was a charismatic preacher and one admirer wrote that 'it was a new

45 *Cartoon by Robert Cruikshank, entitled 'The Oakland Cottages, Cheltenham, or Fox Hunters & their Favourites' (1825), perhaps a comment on the chief preoccupations of Col Berkeley and his cronies. These cottages were near the Prestbury road.*

46 *The Cotswold Hounds and followers of the hunt gathered at the* Rising Sun, *Cleeve Hill in January 1925.*

47 *Cheltenham's last volunteer rifle company, known as E Company, 2nd Gloucestershire Rifle Volunteer Corps, was one of the earliest companies in the country to have a cyclist detachment, shown in this photograph dated 1886-7.*

and interesting sight to see so singularly handsome a young man filled with such religious zeal'. Close was a man of pronounced views, in common with many Evangelical preachers of his day. After his appointment as Perpetual Curate of St Mary's in 1826, he set about regulating life in the town in what one admirer described as a 'despotism of goodness'. He preached for the establishment of new churches and schools, and against gambling, the theatre and Sunday trains, with great energy and determination. He was also strongly opposed to dancing, and in characteristic style said, 'When Mrs Close wished my daughters taught dancing, I reminded her of her marriage vow.' Close's domination of Cheltenham lasted until 1856 when he was appointed Dean of Carlisle.

Col William Fitzhardinge Berkeley was a great social leader in Regency Cheltenham. Prominent in local politics, he also spent much of his life involved in sport and theatricals. He established the Cotswold Hunt, a part of the Berkeley Hunt until 1815, at the *Plough*, setting up the hunt kennels, first in North Street and then in Whaddon Lane. Local saddlers and smiths were

kept busy through the popularity of the sport, and a procession was held through Cheltenham to the sound of church bells at the close of each season. The Berkeley family also set up the Cheltenham Stag Hounds in the town in 1837, with a dozen stable-reared red deer, and the sport remained popular until 1858. Col Berkeley was a generous benefactor, giving £1,000 in 1819 towards maintaining the Races. He kept several mistresses in the town, including the actress Maria Foote, and lent his house, German Cottage, for others to entertain ladies of doubtful reputation.

Many retired military officers in Cheltenham encouraged interest in the defence of the town. In 1795 the increased threat of French invasion led to the formation of the Cheltenham Cavalry Volunteers, who were expected to support King and Country 'at all times and in all places'. Three years later volunteers for the Cheltenham Corps of Infantry, under the command of Sir William Hicks, had a more limited remit, promising only to be 'ready to serve on any occasion when the necessities of the Country may render it necessary at any place within eight miles of Cheltenham'. Both Cavalry and Infantry Volunteers had to provide their own uniform and arms, though this expense was lessened by public subscription. The Infantry Corps was disbanded in 1802, after being thanked by the King, and the Volunteer Cavalry probably did not last beyond Wellington's victory in 1815.

By 1847 there was again concern that France was planning to invade, and 7 Corps, the Gloucestershire Rifle Volunteers, was officially formed at a meeting at Royal Old Wells on 2 June 1859, led by Lord Ellenborough. When Ellenborough

48 *The* Plough, *Cheltenham's main coaching inn for many years, existed under this name as early as 1727, and it is believed that there had been an inn on the site since the 16th century. The building was demolished* c.1982 *to make way for the Regent Arcade.*

49 *The* Queen's Hotel, *originally known as* Liddell's Hotel *after its first licensee, acquired its name at about the time that Queen Victoria was crowned. The* Royal Victoria *and the* Royal Gloucester Hotel *were other names suggested during its development.*

50 *Cartoon by Robert Cruikshank, dated 1824, entitled 'Eccentrics in the High Street, Cheltenham'. It captures the popular image of the town's upper-class residents and visitors. In 1821 William Cobbett described them as 'the lame and lazy, the gourmandising and guzzling, the bilious and nervous'.*

announced in the House of Lords that invasion by France was imminent, the government agreed to supply rifles to the Volunteers, immediately increasing local support, which had been slow at first. Two further corps were quickly set up

51 *Following the demolition of the New Club (site of The Quadrangle) in 1970, part of the decorative canopy over the doorway was re-erected at Belgrave House, now Pizza Express, opposite.*

in Cheltenham – the Cotswold Rifle Volunteers (10 Corps) and a group from the local Friendly Society of Oddfellows (13 Corps). All three corps made use of a shooting range and practice ground at Southam. A fourth corps was formed in 1860 – 14 (Cheltenham) Company. The Volunteers held regular drill practice in Wellington Square and St George's Square. The threatened invasion did not come, and by the summer of 1863 interest in the volunteer movement faded once again. With reduced numbers the corps gradually amalgamated, until by the 1890s there were just two in the area – the Cheltenham Engineer Volunteers and the Gloucestershire Rifle Volunteer Corps. Finally in April 1908 all rifle volunteer battalions across the country became part of the newly formed Territorial Force.

Goding estimated that 2,000 visitors came to Cheltenham in 1800, and local newspapers recorded in great detail the visits of royalty and other notables. The town proved an attractive alternative to Europe during the Napoleonic Wars. The exiled French royal family visited Cheltenham on numerous occasions from May 1811 onwards, taking the waters and visiting the Salts Manufactory on Bath Road. The Duchesse D'Angouleme, only daughter of Louis XVI, and her husband, the Comte D'Artois, stayed at the *York Hotel* in 1811 and at Cambray Lodge in 1813. The couple was thought by many to be the rightful heirs to the French throne, and Goding considered that the French royal family's many visits to Cheltenham proved 'the estimation in which the place [was] held by foreign nations'. The *Clarence Hotel*, originally a boarding house, was renamed in 1827 after the Duchess of Clarence had stayed for a few days, and a royal coat of arms was erected over the Ionic porch of the hotel after the Duchess became Queen Adelaide, wife of William IV.

The *Plough*, Cheltenham's most important coaching inn, was extended to cope with the steadily increasing demand for accommodation. Many private houses were converted into hotels, such as the *Belle Vue Hotel* on the London Road, once home of the Hicks-Beach family. The *Queen's Hotel* was built on the site of Underwood's Sherborne Spa in 1838 at a cost of £47,000. This spectacular four-storey building at the top of the Promenade was designed along classical lines by the Jearrads, and has been compared in style with the Temple of Jupiter in Rome, and to Russian buildings in old St Petersburg. Richard Liddell became the first lessee, paying £2,100 per annum for the 70 bedrooms, 25 sitting rooms, coffee and billiard rooms, and servants' accommodation. Despite its grandeur the hotel did not prosper at first, and major improvements were needed before it overtook the *Plough* as the foremost hotel in Cheltenham.

As the town grew, there was an increasing need for suitable entertainment for the visiting gentry. Cheltenham's newest Assembly Rooms were opened in the High Street, with a grand fête, by the Duke and Duchess of Wellington during

52 *Mawe and Tatlow's Museum, c.1826. John Mawe, a diamond importer and acknowledged expert on mineralogy, published many reference books on these subjects, and is still quoted today. He travelled widely and was the first foreigner permitted to visit the mineral treasures of Brazil.*

53 *After the death of Lord Northwick in 1859, Thirlestaine House became the residence of Sir Thomas Phillipps, who gathered a famous and extensive library, which included a large number of manuscripts relating to Gloucestershire.*

their visit in 1816. 'The first personages of the country, in station, affluence and respectability' were allowed to enter, but the rules stated categorically that 'no person hired or otherwise, in this town or neighbourhood; no person concerned in retail trade; no theatrical or other performers by profession, be permitted'. For the privileged there were weekly subscription balls between November and Easter in the imposing 87ft ballroom, lit by 11 chandeliers, besides concerts and many other entertainments. The Assembly Rooms vied with Montpellier Spa for popularity. In 1826 the Rev. F.E. Witts described the latter as being the place for 'speculating matrons, chaperoning fair and elegant but slenderly endowed nymphs with taper waists, and elderly bachelors from the banks of the Ganges, with injured livers and bilious complexions'.

The Gloucestershire and Cheltenham Club 'for the gentry and nobility of the County of Gloucestershire' was located above the Assembly Rooms. The curry at the Club was said to be the best in England. The Assembly Rooms were demolished in 1900 to make way for Lloyds Bank. The *Imperial Hotel*, built in 1823, became the home of the Imperial Club in 1856 under its chairman William Nash Skillicorne, with membership open to 'resident noblemen and gentlemen'. In 1874 The New Club opened on the corner of the Promenade and Imperial Square. Once again access was restricted to 'visitors of approved rank in society'. Freemasonry had been strong in Cheltenham since 1817, and many officers held positions of influence in the town. Initially members met in *Sheldon's Hotel* in the High Street, but in 1823 a new Masonic Hall was built at the junction of Portland Street and Pittville Street, in the austere style of a Roman mausoleum by architect G.A. Underwood, himself a mason.

Cheltenham residents actively sought to develop the town's reputation as a centre for culture

54 *The Literary and Philosophical Institution, 1840s. In 1860 nearly 1,000 people opposed a plan to turn the magnificent building into a Public Library, with a Corn Exchange and Town Hall behind. Instead H.J. Stucke, a Clarence Street tailor, paid £2,775 for the site, on which he relocated his premises, building two shops and dwellings with workshops to the rear.*

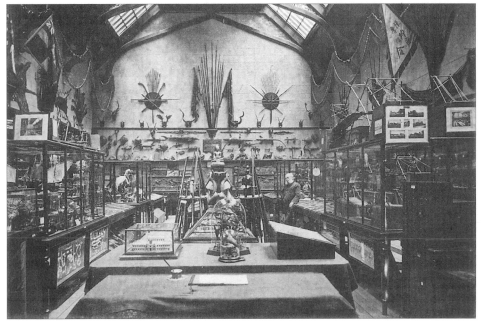

55 *Charles Pierson founded the Cheltenham College Museum in 1870, donating a large collection of geological specimens. The Museum opened in a converted racquet court the following year, later expanding into a second court as the collections increased.*

56 'The Crippetts' drawn by Edward Wilson in 1888, aged 16. Some of Wilson's delicate watercolours, together with artefacts from his Antarctic expeditions, are on permanent display in Cheltenham Art Gallery and Museum.

and learning. In 1810 Jacob Spornberg, a Finnish artist, opened a 'Cheltenham Museum of Natural and Artificial Curiosities' in the High Street. The collection included a display of limewood models made by Spornberg, including one of Pittville Pump Room. Mawe and Tatlow's Museum was opened adjacent to Montpellier Spa in 1816 by John Mawe and his son-in-law Anthony Tatlow. The museum specialised in minerals, replicas of famous vases and models of well-known international landmarks, such as Cleopatra's Needle. The Duke of Wellington would browse around the museum on his way to breakfast during his visit to the town in 1828. Mawe and Tatlow's closed in 1841, and the Montpellier Exchange was built on the site. Thirlestaine House, on Bath Road, was built in 1823, designed by its owner J.R. Scott at a cost of £80,000. Lord Northwick subsequently lived in this princely residence, adding a magnificent gallery, the exterior of which was decorated with antique sculpturing in bold relief. Both house and gallery were crammed with thousands of works of art, including paintings by Holbein and Titian, and the public were encouraged to visit this 'unrivalled

collection' each afternoon between one and four p.m.

In 1833 the Literary and Philosophical Institution was formed in Cheltenham, to counter what one of its founders described as 'watering place imbecility'. (Edward Jenner had observed to a friend in 1805 that there was 'a great dearth of mind' in Cheltenham.) The Institution sought to promote interest in literature and the sciences (then known as 'philosophy') amongst the 'educated visitors, opulent residents, men of talent, of moral respectability [and] of scientific and literary taste'. In 1836 a splendid classical building was erected to house the Institution in the Promenade, designed by R.W. Jearrad in imitation of the Temple of Theseus in Athens. It contained a reading room with a collection of valuable books, and a museum that held many curiosities including a 'perfect Egyptian mummy'. Subscribers could attend lectures on a wide variety of topics between September and May. The annual meeting of the British Society for the Advancement of Science was held at the Institution in 1856, at which Henry Bessemer first announced his process for manufacturing steel inexpensively, later known as the Bessemer Process. The Institution closed in 1860, dogged by financial difficulties and accusations of 'absurd exclusivism'. Its entire collection was transferred to Cheltenham College on condition that it should be opened to the public once a week, free of charge. The size and range of the collection was expanded with the encouragement of the principal, the Rev. Jex-Blake, and the College Museum was opened to the public in 1871. With no other museum in the town at the time, it was attracting 50 visitors each week by the 1880s.

The increase in literacy during the late 18th and early 19th centuries led to a greater demand for books. Initially residents and visitors alike had to make use of private collections, or subscribe to one of the 'literary saloons'. Here they could read London and local newspapers, periodicals and serious works, in order to keep up with the issues of the day, and enjoy the saloons' other function of gossiping-house. In 1826 Cheltenham had six saloons, also known as 'lounge libraries', all situated in or near the High Street. These included Duffield and Weller's, established in 1822; William's, which stood adjacent to the Assembly Rooms for 60 years; and Bettison's, situated further down the same side of the High Street. Many of the saloons were also 'circulating libraries', allowing subscribers to borrow a book or novel for an additional fee, to be read in the privacy of their own home, an arrangement which particularly appealed to women.

57 *Lady Kathleen Scott, widow of Capt. Scott, modelled the bronze statue of Edward Wilson that was unveiled in the Long Garden, the Promenade, in 1914. Scott had described Wilson as 'the best of the comrades and staunchest of friends'. (Photograph by David Kemish.)*

In 1884, after much wrangling, Cheltenham's first Public Library was established in Liverpool Place in the High Street. Unlike earlier libraries it allowed the public access to reading material without subscription. Local architect W.H. Knight designed the imposing library building that was erected at the junction of Clarence Street and St George's Place between 1887-9. The Schools of Art and Science were also situated in upper rooms of the building, before moving to St Margaret's Road in 1905. The Art Gallery, adjacent to the Library, was opened with great ceremony in 1899, and Baron de Ferrieres, the prime mover in its establishment, with a £1,000 contribution, donated 43 pictures by early Dutch artists from his own private collection.

From 1907 onwards the upper rooms at the Art Gallery were occupied by the town's first Public Museum, initially proposed by eminent local physician Edward Thomas Wilson in 1891. Edward's son, Edward Adrian Wilson, known as Ted, was born at the family home in Montpellier Terrace in 1872. Two years later the Wilson family moved to Westal, Montpellier Parade, which remained the family home for the next 56 years. Ted's mother Mary, an acknowledged expert on rearing poultry, practised 'scientific farming' at a small farm near Up Hatherley, and later at The Crippetts on Leckhampton Hill. Ted, an accomplished artist, acquired an intense love of nature during his many visits to The Crippetts, which he described as 'a little piece of heaven'. He followed his father into medicine, and between 1901-4 he was Junior Surgeon and Zoologist with Captain Scott's expedition to the Antarctic. On Ted's return Cheltenham was gripped with Antarctic fever, and in 1905 thousands visited an exhibition of his paintings. In 1910 he became Chief of Scientific Staff, Artist and Zoologist with Scott's second Antarctic expedition, tragically dying with Scott on 12 March 1912, two months after reaching the South Pole.

58 *The interior of St Mary's parish church, looking east. During the rise of the spas the church became desperately overcrowded, despite the addition of wooden galleries that put much strain on the fabric of the building. Consequently the church underwent extensive repairs and restoration during the late 19th century.*

FIVE

Religion and Politics

In medieval times, besides the burden of payments to the manor, Cheltenham residents had to pay tithes to the church, and following a death the heirs had to give their second best beast to the priest. The church was concerned with the moral welfare of the inhabitants, who might be summoned to the Consistory Court of the diocese on committing adultery or slander. Priests were not necessarily without sin themselves, and in 1378 the Bishop of Worcester dismissed the keeper of Cheltenham parish church, Nicholas Fairforde, following his scandalous conduct. Two chantries, of St Katherine and of St Mary, were established at the parish church in the late Middle Ages, the latter by Walter French, a manor bailiff. The endowments of these chantries were confiscated at the Reformation, and granted by Queen Elizabeth in 1574 to Richard Pate, who endowed the free Grammar School and an Almshouse with the funds.

During the reign of the Roman Catholic Queen Mary the former Latin service was briefly restored. At least one religious heretic from Cheltenham was burned at the stake at this time. This was John Coberley (in some sources William), martyred on 24 March 1556, who had been inspired by William Tyndale's translation of the Bible. He was arrested with two Wiltshire men, John Maundrell and John Spicer, while speaking out against the popery practised at the parish church of Keevil, in Wiltshire. The men were imprisoned at Salisbury, where they refused to revoke, John Maundrell

stating that 'wooden images were good to roast a shoulder of mutton, but evil in the church'. Within days they were burned at the stake, and it was noted that John Coberley took a particularly long time to die, his body still moving after the flesh had shrunk from his bones. His wife Alice recanted and was allowed to return home. A Cheltenham Manor Court roll entry dated 17 April 1556 states that John Coberley, who held a message and 13 acres of land in Westal, 'was lately attained and burnt for divers heresies and false opinions … whereby he forfeited his lands to the Lady of the Manor, the Queen'. A note in the margin states that there was no forfeiture in such a case, and Alice, his widow, carried the lands to her second husband, Robert Ible.

Further episodes of religious intolerance occurred, including that concerning John English DD, minister of Cheltenham during the Civil War. He was imprisoned by the Puritans for 18 weeks in 1643 and a monument in the parish church records that this caused the death of his wife, Jane. He was sequestered from his office in 1646 and died the following year. In 1716 Mr Welles of Prestbury, a clergyman and magistrate, recorded in his diary, 'Mary Careless committed to quarter sessions for saying twice King George was a Papist Dog. Mary Hill likewise committed for saying, No, he was a Presbyterian'.

During the Reformation the Crown confiscated the rectory of Cheltenham from Cirencester

59 *The oldest tombstone in the parish churchyard, photographed 300 years after being raised, in 1907. The Machin family were yeomen of Charlton Kings and Cheltenham. The stone can still be seen on the exterior wall of the church next to that of Anthonie's daughter, Anne, who died in 1614.*

green carpet for the communion table bordered with 'needlework of myne owne workinge, and to be trymed with silke frynge'.

The Vestry bought the parish churchyard in 1806 for £100; it had been private property until then, held by the lay impropriator, Joseph Pitt. It was enlarged in 1812 with the purchase of a piece of land in Chester Walk, but this expansion was insufficient and a New Burial Ground was opened in a former orchard off the Lower High Street in September 1831. Part of the Ground was opened as a public garden in 1892, and in 1966 was re-opened as the Sir Winston Churchill Memorial Garden. It was replaced as a burial ground in 1864 when the Improvement Commissioners opened a new town cemetery on an 18-acre plot of land in Bouncer's Lane. W.H. Knight designed the first cemetery buildings, and the Crematorium was officially opened in 1938.

Abbey. It was then granted to a succession of lessees, until Sir Baptist Hicks finally bought it in 1612. Each lessee was bound to maintain the fabric of the chancel, and provide two chaplains and two deacons at his own expense. One lessee was Sir Francis Bacon, who sublet the rectory to Mrs Elizabeth Baghott. She refused to honour her obligations to pay reasonable salaries to the ministers of Charlton Kings and Cheltenham. Although the annual income of the rectory was £400, she paid the two ministers only £10 annually and the lay deacons less than £2 each. In 1610 the Bishop of Gloucester tried unsuccessfully to persuade Mrs Baghott, and the problem continued, despite petitions to the king. After her death in 1622 her sons, John and Thomas Higgs, still refused to pay reasonable stipends until finally compelled by a lawsuit of 1625. Ironically the family did show some interest in the church, as Mrs Baghott's daughter, Anne Higgs, bequeathed ornaments to it including a

60 *This small chapel, in Doric Greek style but with an Egyptian feel, was designed by Rowland Paul to serve the New Burial Ground, opened in 1831 off the Lower High Street.*

61 Holy Trinity Church, Portland Street, drawn by M.D. Eichbaum, c.1840. A goat is depicted standing on the pavement outside the building that housed the Cheltenham Manor Court for many years.

The first Anglican building to supplement the parish church was Holy Trinity, designed by G.A. Underwood and opened in 1823. A further 13 Anglican churches were built in Cheltenham over the next 60 years. Many of these were built on the 'proprietary system', with the majority of pews owned by the 'proprietors' or shareholders who had paid for the building of the church. In an effort to cater for the increasingly disillusioned artisan population, the churches in the poorer areas of town provided mainly free sittings. The first of these was St Paul's (designed by John Forbes in 1827) followed by St Philip's, Leckhampton (opened 1840), serving the Bath Road area, and St Peter's (1849) on the Tewkesbury Road. Five of the churches built in the latter half of the 19th century were designed by the local architect, John Middleton. A temporary corrugated iron church was erected in 1859 to house the congregation during extensive renovation of St Mary's parish church, which was re-opened in 1861. St Matthew's was built on the site of the temporary church in 1879, thanks to the efforts of the Rector of St Mary's, Canon Bell, who proposed that it should replace St Mary's as the parish church, a change which eventually took place towards the end of the 20th century. Three more Anglican churches were opened during the 20th century – Emmanuel (replacing an earlier building in 1936) in Leckhampton, St Aidan's (1959) in Hesters Way, and St Michael's (1966) in Whaddon.

Nonconformists were present in Cheltenham for several centuries. A Quaker community existed in the town as early as 1658, linked to the Society of Friends at Stoke Orchard. Until the Toleration Act of 1689 it was illegal to hold nonconformist religious meetings of more than four people, and in 1684 a number of Cheltenham Friends were

62 *The west door of* All Saints' Church, *carved by R.L. Boulton & Sons. The church, designed by John Middleton, was for High Church, Tractarian worship. Adolph Holst, the father of the composer Gustav Holst, was organist here.*

63 *The first Friends' Meeting House in Cheltenham. This drawing c.1784 appeared in* Thomas Pole M.D. *by E.T. Wedmore, published by the Friends Historical Society, 1908. (Reproduced with the permission of the Religious Society of Friends in Britain.)*

fined or imprisoned for attending Quaker services. One of those imprisoned was Elizabeth Sandford, who granted land to trustees in October 1701 on which to build a Quaker Meeting House. The trustees were William Mason, John Pumfry and John Drewett, and the Meeting House, situated in Manchester Place (now Chelsea Square), was licensed in 1703. William Mason, on whose land the first spa was discovered, was probably one of the first trustees, and his daughter Elizabeth, who married Henry Skillicorne, was buried in the Quaker Burial Ground in Grove Street. This was opened c.1700, but is now a builder's yard, although it is still consecrated ground. A second, more substantial Meeting House was built adjacent to the first in 1836, the façade of which can still be seen in Clarence Street. The Friends moved to a new Meeting House in Portland Street in 1902, until the modern road relief scheme necessitated demolition and the present Meeting House in Warwick Place was built.

The Rev. John Cooper was dismissed as perpetual curate of Cheltenham parish church in 1662, for espousing Unitarian beliefs. He was immediately elected minister of the Unitarian congregation in Cheltenham, serving in that capacity until his death in 1682. The Unitarian Chapel, built in Albion Street in 1662, seated 150 people and is said to have been 'of great antiquity, furnished with a gallery, the pulpit and sitting ornamented with curious carving'. The building closed as a Unitarian Chapel c.1790. Unitarianism was revived in Cheltenham in the early 1830s, and in 1844 a new Chapel was built in Chapel Walk, Bayshill, designed by London architect H.R. Abraham. It was the first building in Cheltenham in Anglo-Norman style, and Goding, who was a member of the congregation, described it proudly as 'an elegant structure'. The chapel is now used as an auction room, and the congregation worships in the former schoolroom.

64 *Wesleyan Methodist Chapel, St George's Street, was one of 100 new chapels built to celebrate the centenary of Methodism. It was opened in 1840, when the Ebenezer Chapel, King Street, had become too small for the congregation, and remained in use by the Methodists until 1971.*

A Baptist congregation meeting was established in Tewkesbury in 1655. This included Cheltenham members who from 1690 held their own meetings in a converted malthouse in Cheltenham. A small Baptist Chapel was opened in 1703 on a plot of land facing St James' Square, purchased from George Forty in 1700. It was replaced by the current building on the site, opened as the Bethel Chapel in 1820 and used by the Baptists until 1951. It was subsequently used by Mormons and Christadelphians.

John Wesley, founder of the Methodist movement, first arrived in Cheltenham on 17 April 1739, describing it as a 'poor, straggling hamlet with a few thatched cottages'. He was refused

*65 Portrait of Robert Capper (1768-1851) by Richard Dighton.
Capper was a wealthy local lawyer, magistrate and JP who lived
at Marle Hill House, Pittville. A considerable benefactor to the
town, Capper was a Calvinist who built the Portland Chapel,
North Place, in 1816 as a place where views similar to his own
could be preached.*

the evangelical Truths of the Gospel'. Initially Lord Dartmouth opened his residence for preaching, but in 1764 the Methodists obtained permission to use a redundant chapel in Albion Street, opposite the present Pate's Almshouses. This chapel had been built *c.*1723 by Mr Millet, a Presbyterian, but closed following his death. In September 1813 the Methodist community opened Ebenezer Chapel in King Street. The trustees included one of the leading local Methodist preachers, Oliver Watts, an ironmonger and bookseller in Cheltenham. At that time the newly formed Cheltenham Circuit had 13 preaching places in the Cheltenham area. A further chapel was opened in St George's Street in 1840.

In the late 1820s the Church of England, Quakers and other Nonconformists agreed to build a shared meeting room in the area south of the town. Straddling the upper Bath Road, and known as Southtown, this self-contained district of shops, tradesmen and artisan dwellings had sprung up in the 1820s. In June 1830 the foundation stone was laid for a small building in Great Norwood Street, initially called the Bethesda Schoolroom as the Quakers would only contribute to a school. This was replaced by the Methodist Bethesda Chapel in 1846. William Moody Bell, whose family established a long-lived surgical supply business in Cheltenham, was one of the Trustees of the Chapel, and was described as one of the 'pillars of the Wesley society'.

On 5 July 1808 the Rev. Rowland Hill, a leading Nonconformist preacher, laid the foundation stone of Cheltenham Chapel in St George's Square before a crowd of about three thousand. The completed chapel opened the following year, with the pulpit available to ministers of various denominations, both Anglican and Nonconformist. In 1813 the congregation settled under the 33-year-long ministry of the Rev. J. Brown. Although services here were conducted on the plan of Lady

permission to use the parish church and instead preached on the bowling green near the *Plough*. The crowd of nearly 2,000 from the surrounding area was said to be 'one of the largest audiences that ever assembled there'. Methodism was permanently established in Cheltenham in 1757 when George Whitefield, a native of Gloucester, was sent by the Countess of Huntingdon to 'spread

Huntingdon's chapels, there was still no chapel in Cheltenham belonging to her Connexion. One had been proposed as early as 1781, but Lady Huntingdon withdrew her interest following the non-compliance of one of her Methodist students in Cheltenham, a Mr Shenstone, who then established a small Baptist congregation. However, in 1816 Robert Capper, of Marle Hill, built the Portland Chapel at his own expense. His appointed minister, Thomas Snow, adopted Strict Baptist views, excluding Capper from his own chapel by only giving Communion to those baptised there. In 1819 Capper presented the chapel to the trustees of Lady Huntingdon's Connexion.

Visitors to Cheltenham c.1800 included many Catholics, particularly of the Irish aristocracy and those who hoped to serve them. St Peter's Catholic Chapel had opened in Gloucester in 1795, and a Gloucester priest would travel to Cheltenham during the summer months to celebrate Mass. The Rev. Nicholas Alexander Cesar Robin, a French language teacher, settled in Cheltenham in 1807. Having been a secular priest of the Diocese of Laon, Abbé Robin began saying Mass in Cheltenham, and was even allowed to use the Town Hall for a year. In October 1809 Dom. John Augustine Birdsall arrived in Cheltenham to look after the local Catholics, sustaining a friendship with the Abbé Robin until the latter's death in 1811. On arrival Father Birdsall used his own money to build a chapel in Somerset Place (corner of St James' Square), celebrating Mass at the *York Hotel* (on the Strand) during its construction. Members of the French royal family worshipped at the chapel during their visits to Cheltenham.

In 1827 Birdsall opened a charity school adjoining the chapel, which moved to St Paul's Street North in 1857, and to its present site in

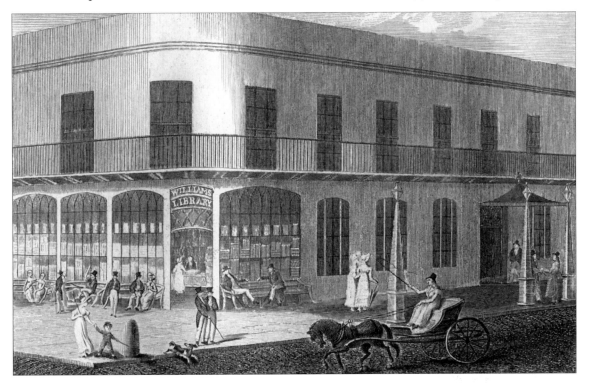

66 *Williams' Library next to the Assembly Rooms, 1826. George Arthur Williams was an influential resident Catholic, becoming High Bailiff of Cheltenham in 1847.*

67 *The interior of the Synagogue, St James' Square, which is said to contain the oldest existing Ashkenazi Synagogue furniture in the United Kingdom. Photographed by Mary Nelson during a visit by the Cheltenham Local History Society in 2003.*

68 *Canvassing in Cheltenham during the 1910 general election. Richard Mathias, a Welsh shipowner, was the Liberal candidate. He proved unsuccessful in the election, possibly as he was not a local man.*

Knapp Road in 1938 as St Gregory's Primary School. Under Francis Close's rule in Cheltenham there was opposition to the Catholic Emancipation Bill of 1829, and a threat to the chapel. Father Birdsall described a contemporary placard which called for 'all true Protestants' to meet and demolish the 'heap of Rubbish that stands in this town near the Baptist Chapel'. The moment passed without incident, although Francis Close preached a sermon against the Roman Catholic Church annually on 5 November from 1839-54. Father Birdsall remained in Cheltenham until 1836 when he left to establish a small monastery at Broadway. A large new church, dedicated to St Gregory and designed in the Decorated Gothic style by Charles Hansom of Clifton, was opened on the site of the Catholic chapel in May 1857. A second church, St Thomas More's, was built in Princess Elizabeth Way in 1967.

A permanent Jewish congregation was established in Cheltenham by 1823, and members met in a rented upper-floor room near the junction of St George's Place and Manchester Walk (now Clarence Street). The following year land was purchased in Elm Street for use as a burial ground. The synagogue, designed by W.H. Knight, was opened in 1839 opposite the Infant School in St James' Square. The New Synagogue, Leadenhall Street, London had donated much of the furniture in 1837 and also supplied the two large decorative prayer panels, probably made for the Great Synagogue, London on the accession of George II in 1727. Cheltenham's small Jewish community included Sir Francis Goldsmidt, who subscribed to the Synagogue from 1865 until his death in 1878. In 1858 he became the first Jewish QC, and was MP for Reading from 1860-78. By 1894 there were no local Hebrew families in the town, most of the congregation consisting of boys from Corinth House, the Jewish Boarding House at Cheltenham College until 1922. The size of the Jewish congregation fluctuated throughout

69 *Harward's Buildings, built in 1822-3 by George Allen Underwood and named after the owner of this part of the Promenade. The Municipal Offices now occupy most of the terrace.*

the 20th century, but continued to thrive with members attending from Gloucestershire and the surrounding counties.

The Evangelist Rev. Francis Close once said, 'there is no distinction between politics and religion'. He and others with a strong influence in Cheltenham, such as Joseph Pitt, were staunch Conservatives, while the Nonconformists tended to support the Liberal cause. One notable Whig in Cheltenham was Col William Fitzhardinge Berkeley, whose views and morals were anathema to Close. With the Reform Bill of 1832 Cheltenham became a parliamentary borough, able to return its first Member of Parliament since Elizabeth I had excused the town the expense of sending a representative to London. The Hon. Craven Berkeley, youngest brother of the colonel, was returned unopposed as Liberal Member, and for many years afterwards Cheltenham was a Liberal stronghold. When the Conservative *Cheltenham Journal* carried implied criticism of Col Berkeley's private life, the Colonel enlisted the help of two friends and horsewhipped the editor in his own home in Northfield Place. Berkeley subsequently had to pay the editor £500 damages, but some years later brought a successful libel action against another Conservative newspaper, the *Cheltenham Chronicle*. The Liberals kept an almost unbroken hold on Cheltenham until 1885, after which the Conservatives held power for the next 20 years. The town remained a Tory stronghold during much of the 20th century, the last Conservative MP being Charles Irving who served until 1992. In 1980 the Liberals became the majority party on the Borough Council after a lapse of 76 years, and in 1992 Nigel Jones was elected Liberal Democrat MP for Cheltenham.

The 1832 Reform Bill failed to improve the political position of most working men, resulting in widespread support for the People's Charter in 1838. This demanded the abolition of the property qualification to vote, allowing voting rights to all men, not just the wealthy. Chartist followers in Cheltenham were said to be mostly shoemakers, tailors, gardeners and cabinetmakers, and were led by blacksmith J.P. Glenister. A Chartist meeting in Montpellier Gardens in 1852 attracted 2,000 people, and Chartist pamphlets and ballads, published by Cheltenham printer Thomas Willey, were widely circulated. An alarmed resident declared that the Chartists were 'making politicians of the agricultural labourers', but W.E. Adams, a central figure in the local movement, described local supporters as 'earnest and reputable people' rather than violent radicals. Liberal politicians such as Berkeley recognised that Chartist supporters, despite having few votes, were numerous enough to make their favour worth cultivating.

Elections in the town were rowdy affairs during the 19th century. Candidates paid the fares for their voters to attend, and plied them with drink and large dinners. Rival supporters would throw missiles, including eggs and dead cats, at the speakers, and in the excitement of the 1865 election a Conservative supporter, John Glasse, shot dead William Lynes, a Berkeley supporter. Unlike today, the elections affected the whole town, as shown in the Christ Church Infants' School logbook entry for 17 November 1868: 'A very small School in the afternoon, very many being taken by their friends to the Election, and some afraid to come out.' Although Cheltenham gained the right to elect its own MP in 1832, it was not until September 1876 that it became an incorporated borough, by virtue of a Royal Charter. The Borough Council, led by a Mayor, replaced the Town Commissioners, and the present system of local government was introduced. The Borough coat of arms was granted in 1887, and since 1914 the Municipal Offices have been housed in part of Harward's Buildings in the Promenade.

SIX

Foundations of Knowledge

As early as 1417, in a Cheltenham Manor Court roll entry of 10 March, one tenant's occupation is given as 'scolsmaster' (schoolmaster). The earliest known school in Cheltenham was a grammar school in the Chantry of St Katherine, in St Mary's parish church, probably held in the north aisle. In 1547 Edward VI's Chantry Commissioners recorded that the chantry priest, Edward Grove, was to be paid an annual salary of £5 to teach the children of the parishioners of the market town 'whereunto is no school kept'.

Richard Pate was born in Cheltenham in 1516, the son of Walter and Alice Pate. The family was moderately wealthy, and Walter is recorded in the Manor Court rolls of the 1520s as owner of several parcels of copyhold land, and involved in several trades. Richard probably attended the St Katherine's chantry school before entering Corpus Christi College, Oxford, aged sixteen. After legal training at Lincoln's Inn, he returned to Gloucestershire, eventually becoming Recorder of Gloucester and a member of the Chantry Commission, recording chantry property in the county for confiscation. In 1572 Richard Pate began constructing a new grammar school building in the High Street. Two years later Elizabeth I granted him lands from the old chantry estates, which he used to endow the re-established grammar school. It opened to 50 pupils under the first master, Christopher Ocland. In 1585, three years before his death, Richard Pate established the Pate Foundation, entrusting the Grammar School and Almshouses to Corpus Christi College, Oxford.

The Grammar School suffered a period of closure from 1841-53 following a serious decline. This was largely due to neglect under the trustee-ship of Corpus Christi, as for many years they had not fully applied the endowment income to the school. The school re-opened on 1 May 1853 under a revised scheme sanctioned by the Court of Chancery. In July 1905 the Pate Foundation was enlarged to incorporate the County High as Pate's Grammar School for Girls. The girls' school was held in Livorno Lodge, St Margaret's Road until 1939, when a new site was found in Albert Road where it remained until 1985. In 1965 the boys' Grammar School moved out to Hesters Way, after nearly 400 years in the High Street, and in 1985 it amalgamated with the girls' Grammar to become the present Pate's Grammar School. Famous Old Grammarians include Sir Benjamin Baker, the engineer who designed the Forth Bridge, Sir Rowland Biffen, a respected agriculturist and pioneer in genetics, Brian Jones, the Rolling Stone, Pat Smythe, the show jumper, writers Sylvia Clayton and Sue Limb, and Dame Felicity Lott, the opera singer.

During the 1760s the Grammar School was threatened by competition from a private academy, run by Nonconformist Samuel Wells, whose curriculum better prepared pupils for trade and business. Chester, the Master of the Grammar

School, attempted to have the rival school closed as Wells, described as a 'violent Methodist', did not have the necessary bishop's licence to teach. The private school was probably not very lucrative for Samuel Wells, a Wesleyan minister from 1769-80, as an advertisement in the *Gloucester Journal* in 1753 reveals that he vacated his original house for his brother Joseph, hat-maker, removing the school to the 'Back-side' of town. However, it operated until his death in 1780, attracting the children of spa visitors wishing to 'avoid losing time in their education'. There were many private academies in Cheltenham throughout the 19th century, and an abundance of teachers of art, music, dancing and languages.

In his will of 1683 George Townsend, an Old Grammarian and successful lawyer, provided elementary schooling in Cheltenham for the children of the poor 'to avoid their being offensive at home or elsewhere'. His charity school was re-established in 1713 by a group of subscribers led by the Rev. Francis Welles, Vicar of Prestbury, and the Rev. Henry Mease, incumbent of Cheltenham and Master of the Grammar School. It opened

70 *An austere portrait of Richard Pate from a report, published 1852, which reviewed the reasons for the decline of the Grammar School. The portrait, from a woodcut, is probably much older.*

on 14 November 1713 at a house in the High Street, rented from Thomas Smith. Five years later the Charity School was endowed with a generous bequest from Lady Capel, widow of the Baron of Tewkesbury. Despite this it was removed to a small room above the parish church porch in 1729. Still there in the 1830s, the boys had to carry their elderly schoolmaster, John Garn, up the narrow steps to this schoolroom. Initially the charity schoolboys wore blue coats, yellow stockings, caps and bands. They were paid a small amount for spinning the wool and knitting their own stockings. In 1847 the old Charity School moved to a purpose-built school in Devonshire Street, becoming

71 *German Cottage, built by 1815, was extended and renamed Livorno Lodge later in the 19th century. The house, situated on St Margarets Road, became Pate's Grammar School for Girls (seen here in 1926) and subsequently Richard Pate Junior School, until replaced by the Pate Court office block in the 1980s.*

FIELD HOUSE
ESTABLISHMENT FOR YOUNG LADIES, PRESTBURY, NEAR CHELTENHAM.
CONDUCTED BY THE MISS ASHWINS

Printed & Published by S.Y.Griffith & C?, Cheltenham.

72 *An advertisement dated 1826 for the private academy at Field House (now The Lindens), Prestbury, run by the Misses Ashwin. From 1843-5 the house provided lodgings for those attending the Prestbury Hydropathic Establishment at Sans Souci House (later Morningside).*

the new National School known as the St Mary's Parish Boys' School. This building was converted for residential use in 1992.

Towards the end of the 18th century there was an increasing need for literate workers and accurate clerks. There was also a widespread evangelical desire to educate the masses so that they could be encouraged to live by Christian values. Robert Raikes, the Anglican prison reformer in Gloucester, promoted Sunday Schools as a means of educating the 'ignorant, profane, filthy and disorderly' children who swarmed through the streets every Sunday, unchecked by their parents who were 'totally abandoned themselves'. The idea spread rapidly, and as early as 1787 the first Sunday Schools were opened in Cheltenham, teaching reading, spelling and the Catechism.

There was no schooling for Cheltenham children on weekdays until 30 years later, when elementary education was introduced for those over the age of six. The main educational agency of the Church of England, the National Society, was founded in 1811, and in June 1816 Cheltenham's first National School was established at the old Town Hall in Regent Street. In 1817 the first purpose-built National School building was erected in the town, financed by voluntary subscription (principally from collections after special sermons) and by grants from the Society. The building in Bath Road (now St Luke's Parish Hall) was opened by Dr Andrew Bell, whose monitorial system had been adopted by the Society. This system used older child monitors to teach the younger children, allowing a single schoolteacher to manage

73 *The small room above the north porch of the parish church housed the Charity School for almost 120 years. The opening into the main body of the church was created in 1890.*

a large number of pupils. Dr Bell retired to live in Cheltenham, dying at his home at Lindsay Cottage, Oriel Road, in 1832. By the end of the 19th century every Anglican church in Cheltenham had opened a National School of its own.

Nonconformists in Cheltenham provided elementary education through Chapel Sunday Schools, and the first of their day schools, known as British Schools, was opened in a Sunday School room beneath the Methodist Chapel in North Place in 1820. Two further British Schools were opened in 1843, at the Wesleyan Chapel in St George's Street and the Congregational Chapel in Grosvenor Street. All were run along similar lines to the National Schools, and also used the monitorial system. It was not until 1859 that the North Place Chapel School moved to a purpose-built building in Dunalley Street. Both the National and British Schools were maintained through local effort and were constantly in financial difficulty. In 1845 the Rev. Bellairs, the first School Inspector in Gloucestershire, deplored the lack of support in funding the schools. He claimed that tenant farmers in particular feared that 'instead of a plodding, hard-working peasantry, who do their labour much as the animals they tend, we shall have an effeminate class of persons, averse to rough work, conceited and insubordinate'. It was not until 1880 that elementary school attendance nationally became compulsory up to the age of ten.

In 1823 Samuel Wilderspin, an untrained teacher based in Spitalfields, London, published *On the Importance of Educating the Infant Poor* in which he wrote that a teacher had to become a child himself in order to be successful. It was a revolutionary concept in education. The following year Wilderspin became a travelling missionary for the newly formed Infant School Society, whose aim was to promote the education of children aged between 18 months and seven years, thus saving them from a life of vice and crime. Having read Wilderspin's book, Francis Close announced, in his first sermon as Rector of Cheltenham, that he intended opening an Infant School. He invited Wilderspin to Cheltenham to establish what was to be one of the first Infant Schools in Gloucestershire. Funds were raised to build a small school in Alstone Lane, with the voluntary help of local farmers, while 'the poor gave shrubs and plants for the playground'. The school was officially opened in April 1827 with about 100 pupils, and a

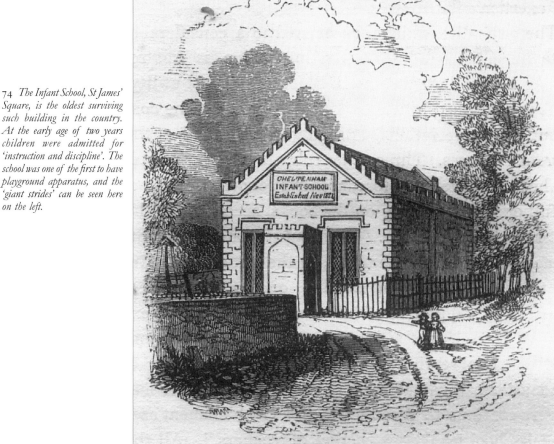

74 *The Infant School, St James' Square, is the oldest surviving such building in the country. At the early age of two years children were admitted for 'instruction and discipline'. The school was one of the first to have playground apparatus, and the 'giant strides' can be seen here on the left.*

month later the public was encouraged to view their progress. The *Cheltenham Chronicle* reported that 'the alphabet, the pence table and other arithmetic rules [were] all put in rhyme and set to popular tunes', and the infants' answers to questions put to them by Mr Wilderspin 'excited much interest' amongst the crowds that had gathered to watch.

The experiment in Alstone was a great success and by 1830 Francis Close had raised sufficient funds to build a second school in St James' Square, accommodating about 300 infants. The school flourished and soon became one of the diversions for visitors to the spa. However, the school was run largely using the monitorial system, with

a curriculum based on the Scriptures, and was condemned by Wilderspin, who had not been consulted on its construction or staffing, as a travesty of infant school practice. Great animosity developed between Close and Wilderspin. Defiantly Wilderspin set up an Infant School Depot at his home in Alpha House in St George's Road (formerly Jenner's vaccination clinic), supplying infant schools across the country with books and equipment. He continued travelling the British Isles, lecturing on infant education and founding new schools. His association with Cheltenham ended in 1839 when he was appointed master of the Central Model School in Dublin, but his

Drawn by W. C. Robson,   Cheltenham.

The Higher Grade!—What we must expect.

First Boy: I say, kid, I'll play thee marbles, twosies up!
Second Boy: I could not think of doing such a thing. I go to Christ Church Schools.

influence continued, and by 1846 there were five infant schools in the town, and many more in Gloucestershire.

By 1900 Cheltenham had begun to pay the price of being a pioneer in education. Elementary provision was scattered amongst 28 small church schools, often in cramped, ageing accommodation. Following the Education Act of 1902, the newly formed Cheltenham Education Committee began rationalising them. For some time, the Church School Managers found it hard to accept the new situation, resenting the loss of influence over the schools that they had established and funded for so long. Despite their opposition the first purpose-built, state-run school was opened in Gloucester Road in 1907.

The Mechanics' Institute, founded under the patronage of a small group of mainly middle-class radicals, was first opened at the old Presbyterian Chapel in Albion Street in 1834, to spread 'knowledge among the trading and mechanical portions' of the town. Members were largely small shopkeepers, nonconformist ministers and men

76 Gloucester Road Council School prior to its opening in 1907. The distinctive 'dragon and onion' lamp standard outside the school was one of those designed for Cheltenham by the Borough Engineer, Joseph Hall.

77 *St Mary's Hall (later Shaftesbury Hall) housed the Female Department of the Teacher Training College from 1869.*

with progressive views. None of them would have been permitted to attend lectures at the Literary and Philosophical Institute. Weekly talks were intended to impart 'useful knowledge', covering a wide range of subjects from geology to infant education. Although initially it had a 'no politics and no religion' rule, the Institute provided an ideal forum for increasingly political topics. In his lectures the local radical William Penn Gaskell called for universal suffrage, urging both men and women to help themselves through temperance and education.

In 1839 the Church of England established the Working Men's Association in rooms in St George's Place as a 'literary and scientific institution for the humbler classes' with Francis Close as President. The Association was presumably set up to help counter the Chartist political influence of

the Mechanics' Institute. In 1843 Henry Davies, in his book *A View of Cheltenham in its Past and Present State,* wrote disparagingly that the Institute still had 'a nominal existence in Albion Street, but its profound objects have been, of late, so perverted to political purposes, that it now scarcely deserves to be catalogued at all among places of scientific or literary instruction'. It is thought that the Mechanics' Institute closed in the mid-1840s.

The Mechanics' Institute and the Working Men's Association provided virtually the only routes by which working-class adults could improve themselves during the early 19th century. Later in the century evening classes performed the same function for both adults and children, providing education without interfering with their working day. In 1871, 70 pupils over the

78 *Cheltenham College, 1889. The buildings were designed in Gothic style by James Wilson of Bath. The chapel on the right, designed by D.J. Humphris, was added in 1858.*

age of 14 were taught drawing, Latin, arithmetic, orthography and spelling for two pence per week at the Christ Church Night School, held in the church schoolroom. The *Cheltenham Examiner* proposed a practical prize system: 'Let a pair of strong double-soled boots, or jacket, or cap, be announced as prizes to the most punctual, and no parent would be found keeping his child at home on frivolous pretexts!'

Francis Close was largely instrumental in the foundation of the Teacher Training College in Cheltenham, established on strict 'Scriptural, Evangelical and Protestant principles'. The Normal College, as it was originally known, opened in June 1847 in two rented rooms with seven male students. It was only the sixth Anglican training college for elementary school teachers in the country. Some considered it a 'hazardous experiment' when 12 women joined the following year, despite the women having their own lecturers, a separate residence in Monson Avenue, and a

garden that the men were forbidden to enter. The Earl of Shaftesbury laid the foundation stone of S.W. Daukes' substantial Tudor Gothic College buildings in Swindon Road on 19 April 1849. Miss Jane Cooke, a local resident, generously donated the five-acre site.

The Female Department was housed in the former High Street Hospital building (now Normandy House) and at the Priory, before moving to the purpose-built St Mary's Hall in St George's Place in 1869. By 1886 the Department was considered to be 'in some respects at the head of all the Female Training Colleges in the Kingdom'. Despite this it was not until 1908 that a Miss Armstrong became the first woman student to obtain a London BA degree through the College. In 1921 the Female Department became a College in its own right, called St Mary's College of Education, and moved to The Park. St Paul's College of Education took over St Mary's Hall, renaming it Shaftesbury Hall (now Chelsea

Square). The two colleges re-combined to become the College of St Paul's and St Mary's in 1979, and in 1990 merged with part of Gloucestershire College of Art and Technology (GlosCAT) to become Cheltenham and Gloucester College of Higher Education. In 2001 the College became the University of Gloucestershire.

With the decline of the Grammar School in the first half of the 19th century there was a clear need for suitable education for the sons of gentlemen, to prepare them for university or a career in the services. A group of local residents, mainly military men and clergy, led of course by Francis Close, established the first of the country's Victorian public schools. Cheltenham College opened in July 1841 in rented houses in Bayshill Terrace, with 120 boys. At first it was a Proprietary College, financed by the sale of shares, with each shareholder entitled to nominate a pupil. It was an immediate success, and in 1843, when the number of pupils had already doubled, the College moved to new buildings in the Bath Road. In the 1860s, with over 700 boys, the school was second only to Eton in size. The College expanded with the addition of D.J. Humphris' chapel building of 1858, the Gymnasium and rackets courts of 1865, and H.A. Prothero's chapel of 1896. A Junior Department opened in the 1860s, later to move across Thirlestaine Road to the grounds of Lake House, once the home of Mourdant Ricketts, a retired indigo planter. The College has continued to flourish and in recent years has become co-educational.

The Ladies' College opened at Cambray House in February 1854. It was established along similar lines to Cheltenham College, whose Principal, the Rev. W. Dobson, was one of the co-founders. Not surprisingly, Francis Close was the first President of the Ladies' College Council. It was under the second Principal, Dorothea Beale, who took over in 1858, that the College became a powerful influence in the development of women's education. At that time it was felt that girls had no need to learn subjects such as science or mathematics. Apparently Miss Beale would say, 'Parents thought their daughters would be turned into boys if they learnt Euclid, but they never minded their learning geometry!' She introduced all stages of education, including a kindergarten and a teachers' training department, one of the first training colleges for secondary school teachers. By 1864 external examiners set and marked the school examinations, and the first University Examiner of Mathematics was the Rev. Charles Dodgson, better known as Lewis Carroll. Miss Beale also pioneered the preparation of women for university degrees and established St Hilda's College, Oxford for women.

79 *Dorothea Beale, 1859, aged 27. One of her earliest pupils described her 'slight, young figure, the very gentle, gliding movements, the quiet face with its look of intense thoughtfulness, ... the wonderful eyes with their calm outlook and expression of inner vision', a description that later pupils might not have recognised.*

80 *A new Science Wing at the Cheltenham Ladies' College was opened in May 1905, completing the fourth side of The Quadrangle.*

81 *Dean Close School in 1901, from the south across Shelburne Road.*

In 1889 she opened St Stephen's Infant School, in Tivoli, as a practising school for her trainee kindergarten teachers. John Ruskin was a friend and supporter of Miss Beale, and presented several valuable books and manuscripts to the College.

Pupil numbers greatly increased under Miss Beale and in 1873 the Ladies' College moved from Cambray House to the Victorian Gothic buildings in St George's Road designed by John Middleton. The College continued to expand, first along Montpellier Street, and then Bayshill Road. The Princess Hall was opened in 1897 on the site of Samuel Onley's Royal Well Music Hall, covering the site of the original mineral spring. Recent building includes a new Art and Technology wing in Bayshill Road behind Fauconberg House, opened in 1999. With its excellent reputation, the Ladies' College has been emulated the world over.

Dean Close School opened in Shelburne Road in 1886 in buildings designed by the local architect W.H. Knight. It was established on Evangelical principles as a counterbalance to the two earlier public schools, which had been founded by High Church Tractarians. The school was named as a memorial to Francis Close, who, as Dean of Carlisle, had died in 1882. The first headmaster was the Rev. W.H. Flecker, father of the poet James Elroy Flecker. Under his energetic leadership the school increased in size from an initial 12 boys to 200. Flecker preferred to keep the boys together as a single community in the main building, unlike Cheltenham's other two public schools, and it was only after his retirement in 1924 that the house system was introduced. As the 20th century progressed Dean Close School expanded, becoming co-educational in 1969.

SEVEN

Cultural Connections

Amongst the many well-known cultural figures who visited Cheltenham was composer George Frederick Handel, who first stayed in the town in 1744. He returned in June 1751 at the age of 66 for a rest cure, hoping to curb the loss of sight that was to cut short his career. He probably stayed at the Great House, now the site of St Matthew's Church. At the time of his second visit he was writing his last major work, the oratorio *Jephtha*. In June 2001 Cheltenham celebrated the 250th anniversary of Handel's visit with a concert of his work, which included this rarely performed piece.

Dr Samuel Johnson is known to have stayed in Cheltenham in 1749 and in articles written for *The Rambler* he frequently referred to the scenery around the town, indicating subsequent visits. William Shenstone, pastoral poet, renowned landscape gardener and friend of Johnson, first visited Cheltenham in 1734. On his second visit in 1743 Shenstone fell in love with a young lady in the town, but felt he was not good enough for her. His best-known work *Pastoral Ballad*, said to be 'perhaps the best of its kind in the language', was published in 1755, and was enigmatically dedicated to 'Miss C.', the object of his unrequited love.

The writer Fanny Burney visited Cheltenham with the royal party in 1788 as lady-in-waiting to Queen Charlotte. She wrote an account of the 'Cheltenham episode' in her diary which includes a description of their departure: 'All Cheltenham was drawn out into the High Street, the gentles on one side and the commons on the other.' Another celebrated female writer, Jane Austen, visited Cheltenham for three weeks in May 1816 in an attempt to cure her declining health, thought to be due to breast cancer. Her sister Cassandra accompanied her, but remained longer, and in September the same year Jane wrote to Cassandra via 'The Post Office, Cheltenham' imploring her to return home: 'While the waters agree, everything else is trifling.' Jane died only ten months after her visit to the town.

Lord Byron visited Cheltenham at the age of 13 with his socialite mother in the summer of 1801 and again in 1802. In August 1812, following the end of his passionate affair with Lady Caroline Lamb, he returned to Cheltenham, taking the medicinal waters 'because they were sufficiently disgusting', and claiming that they had disordered him to his 'heart's content'. In early September he moved from 'the sordid Inn' in the High Street (now *The Strand* bar) to Georgiana Cottage, on the corner of Bath Street, Cambray. Byron was a frequent guest at Berkeley Castle with other great dramatists and literary figures of the day. Ireland's national poet Thomas Moore, friend and contemporary of Byron and Shelley, knew Cheltenham well, particularly its Irish residents. Following Byron's death in 1824 Moore received his memoirs but, according to some sources, burned them, presumably to protect his friend's reputation. Moore visited the town many times,

82 *The Great House was converted into a boarding house after the death of Lady Stapleton, becoming the scene of the principal amusements of the day – dancing, cards and tea-drinking – every evening except Monday, until superseded by the Assembly Rooms. The boarding house closed in 1838.*

83 *No. 10 St James' Square, where Tennyson stayed with his mother and sisters. While in Cheltenham he preferred the company of a few close friends, including the poet Sydney Dobell, the Rev. William Dobson, Cheltenham College Principal 1844-9, and Frederick Robertson, Curate of Christ Church, who became a celebrated preacher.*

most notably while collecting material for his own two-volume biography, *Letters and Journals of Lord Byron*, published in 1830.

In 1844 Alfred Lord Tennyson was persuaded to invest the family fortune, and the earnings from his poetry, in woodcarving machinery. Unfortunately, within months the venture had failed, and Tennyson was left penniless and suffering from severe hypochondria. At that time his mother and sisters were renting a house at 10 St James' Square, and Tennyson was recommended to take the waters to restore his health. He avoided the fashionable side of the town, describing it as 'a polka, parson-worshipping place of which Francis Close is Pope'. Despite his disparaging remarks, he used his mother's house as a base for six years, and it is thought that he wrote much of his epic poem 'In Memoriam' there. When the poem was published in 1850 he succeeded Wordsworth as Poet Laureate.

World-famous violinist Paganini had a fanatical following in the early 19th century and nearly 800 people attended each of his two performances at the Assembly Rooms in July 1831. He was persuaded to play a third concert at the Theatre Royal for 200 guineas. This additional concert was intended primarily for the 'lower orders', who were not permitted to enter the Assembly Rooms. However, the nobility and gentry condemned the concert and few of the expensive seats (on which his fee depended) were sold. As a result Paganini refused to play. Angrily, the audience marched to the *Plough*, where it was announced that the violinist would play after all and that his fee would be given to Cheltenham's poor. Some of the crowd returned to the theatre, greeting his performance enthusiastically, but he was later condemned for his 'paltry double-dealing and ingratitude' towards the townspeople. Other great performers who appeared at the Assembly Rooms included Johann

84 The Belle Vue Hotel, *seen here from Berkeley Street c.1846, was originally the town house of the Hicks family.*

85 *Photograph of Alice Liddell, model for her namesake in* Alice's Adventures in Wonderland, *taken by Lewis Carroll in the 1860s.*

The Rev. Charles Dodgson, better known as writer Lewis Carroll, came to Cheltenham in 1863, primarily on business at the Ladies' College. He stayed at the *Belle Vue Hotel*, visiting the Rev. and Mrs Henry Liddell at Hetton Lawn, Cudnall Street in Charlton Kings. Alice Liddell, who was staying with her grandparents at the time, inspired Carroll to write *Alice's Adventures in Wonderland*, published in 1865. It is said that a mirror in the Liddells' home inspired Carroll's second book *Through the Looking Glass*. Fascinated by puzzles and illusions, Carroll noted in his diary that had seen a performance by 'Herr Dobler, a conjurer' while in Cheltenham, and this was possibly echoed in his writing. Dobler was the stage name of George Buck, a pupil of the illusionist Professor Pepper, who was performing his famous 'Pepper's Ghost' illusion at the Assembly Rooms that week. After his visit to Cheltenham Carroll added two further chapters to *Alice's Adventures in Wonderland*, most significantly 'Pig and Pepper' which included the Cheshire Cat which 'vanished quite slowly, beginning with the end of the tail, and ending with the grin' – a description which has strong parallels with Pepper's illusion.

Christina Rossetti, one of the most important Victorian women poets, visited her maternal uncle, Henry Polydore, a solicitor's clerk in Cheltenham and Gloucester, on a number of occasions. Henry, a Roman Catholic, had married Henrietta Mayer, the daughter of a Cheltenham baker, and they had a daughter, also Henrietta. Mrs Polydore left her family while her daughter was still very young and lived apart from them, running a bakery in Bath Road. She became a Mormon and emigrated to America in 1855, taking her daughter with her. While staying with her uncle at Chester Villa, Painswick Road in 1864, Christina Rossetti wrote, 'Cheltenham proper is still, as it was last year, not to my taste, but the environs afford charming drives, and some of the finest views I know.'

Strauss (1838), Liszt (1840), Jenny Lind (1856, 1862) and Paderewski (1893, 1895).

'Rarely have I seen such a place that so attracted my fancy,' Charles Dickens wrote to his actor-manager friend William Charles Macready, who had retired in 1860 to live at 6 Wellington Square. Dickens always included Cheltenham on his reading tours of provincial theatres, and is known to have stayed with Macready several times during the 1860s. Macready, a celebrated Shakespearean actor, also lectured and read aloud in the town. He lived in Cheltenham until his death in 1867.

86 *Chester Villa, Painswick Road, once home of Christina Rossetti's uncle, Henry Polydore. Henry, an articled clerk, chose to anglicise his name from Polidori to Polydore in the hope of attracting wealthy clients. However, according to Christina's brother, William Rossetti, 'the clients never came'. Henry Polydore died at 8 St James' Parade (now Suffolk Parade) in 1885.*

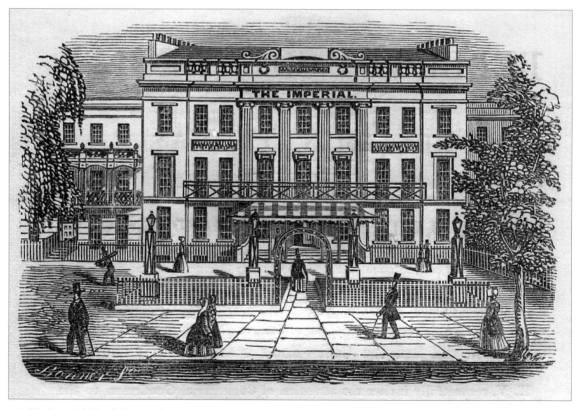

87 *The* Imperial Hotel, *Promenade, c.1851, formerly the home of the artist Hamlet Millet. The hotel subsequently became the Imperial Club and then the town's main Post Office from 1876-1987. It has since been converted into a shop.*

88 *Domenico Barnett, son of the composer John Barnett. Domenico was a talented musician who taught piano at all levels to Ladies' College pupils for 44 years before his death in 1911. His two sisters became well-known singers; Clara Kathleen (later Rogers) moved to the USA where she published musical pieces and several books about singing.*

Several well-known artists and writers became residents of Cheltenham, perhaps attracted by the town's cultural connections. Nathaniel Thomas Haynes Bayly, author, poet and prolific songwriter, described as the 'founder of a new style of English ballads', was living at Oxford Villa, London Road by 1828. He died in the town in April 1839 and was buried in St Mary's churchyard. His mother erected a memorial to him in St James' Church.

In 1823 fashionable English portrait and miniature painter, Hamlet Millet, occupied a newly built house on the west side of the Promenade. It was extravagantly claimed that he was the only artist to discover the methods by which 'Titian and other celebrated masters of the old Venetian school conveyed their colours to the canvas'. After seeing a performance of *Aladdin* in the town, Millet claimed that he had written the play; he had sent his manuscript to the producer for assessment but it had never been returned. Intriguingly, the play's producer is said to have sent Mr Millet a cheque for 100 guineas, followed by further substantial payments.

English composer John Barnett was born in Bedford of Prussian parents (family name Beer). His best-known piece, *Mountain Sylph*, was hailed as the first modern English opera when it was performed at the Lyceum, London in August 1834. In 1841 Barnett moved to Cheltenham where he became a successful singing master at the Ladies' College soon after it opened. He published two books on singing techniques and wrote about 4,000 songs, amongst many other musical pieces. He died at his home, 'Cotteswold' on Leckhampton Hill, in 1890.

The Dightons were amongst the most notable artistic families in England during the Regency period and three generations specialised in small, full-length, humorous cartoons of prominent contemporary personalities in profile. Richard Dighton first came to Cheltenham in 1828, returning in 1832, and painted many of Cheltenham's best-known residents and visitors in the distinctive Dighton style over the next eight years.

The first photographer in Cheltenham was John Palmer, who opened his Photographic Institution in the Promenade in September 1841, one of the earliest provincial studios in the country. It was later run by Richard Beard, whose father (also called Richard) had established Europe's first public photographic studio at the Royal Polytechnic Institution, London in March 1841. There was a dramatic rise in the demand for cheap portraits and *cartes-de-visite* and by 1865 there were 17 photographers in the town.

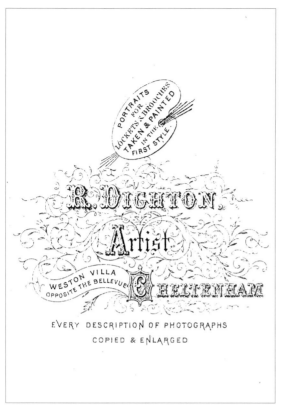

89 Richard Dighton Jnr, son of the artist, opened a photographic studio in the High Street in 1865.

George Rowe was one of the most prolific 19th-century English topographical print-makers, producing more than 650 lithographs between 1823 and 1850, many of which he printed and published himself. Born in Exeter, Rowe moved to Cheltenham in 1832 and established a Repository of Arts at which he sold prints and artists' materials. Over the next 20 years he produced at least 129 lithograph views of Gloucestershire, about half of which were of Cheltenham, as well as views of Devon, Derbyshire, Dorset, and County Wicklow in Ireland. He also lithographed and printed the work of other artists, including that of his wife Philippa and of Richard Dighton. Rowe invested in local ventures, becoming printer and publisher of the *Cheltenham Examiner* newspaper in 1841. In 1848 he purchased the Royal Old Well with

architect Samuel Onley, developer of much of the Bayshill estate. The Royal Well project was a financial disaster and in a desperate attempt to recover his losses Rowe borrowed £73 for passage to Australia to join the gold rush in 1852, leaving his wife and children in England. His fortunes in Australia fluctuated but he continued to paint, commissioned by the British Government to complete watercolour drawings of the Victorian gold fields. He returned to England in 1859 and died in Exeter in 1864.

In August 1914 French sculptor Auguste Rodin was persuaded by his friend, Mlle Judith Cladel, to escape the German invasion of Paris by coming to Cheltenham where her sisters lived. Rodin lived simply at *Sussex House*, a small hotel in Winchcombe Street, and could regularly be seen visiting the Town Hall for news of the war, walking in Pittville Park or studying artefacts in the museum. He stayed for a total of six weeks. Following his death, the most famous version of his white marble sculpture 'The Kiss' was put up for auction in 1929. It failed to meet its reserve price and a few years later was offered on loan to any provincial gallery that could meet the cost of transport and insurance. Cheltenham took up the offer and in 1933 the 4½-ton sculpture was transported to the town for the princely sum of £29 18s. It was exhibited in Cheltenham Art Gallery for six years, before being loaned by Rodin's executors to the Tate Gallery in London. In 1952 the Tate bought 'The Kiss' for the nation following a public appeal. The sculpture is now displayed at Tate Modern.

Cecil Day Lewis, poet and writer, became an English master at Cheltenham College Junior School in 1930, writing detective stories under the pseudonym Nicholas Blake to help pay for repairs to the roof of his home, Box Cottage in Charlton Kings. The first, *A Question of Proof*, was in the thinly disguised setting of the College and

90 *Rodin's marble statue, 'The Kiss', being removed from Cheltenham Art Gallery in February 1939. It was placed in the Tate Gallery, London the following day.*

revolved around an affair between two people at the school. The story was looked on with disapproval by College authorities and he resigned in 1938. Police records from 1933 reveal that Day Lewis had been under surveillance by Gloucestershire police because of suspected communist sympathies, but was later cleared of the charge by MI5. He is remembered by ex-College Junior pupils for always wearing a red tie and for his deadly aim with the blackboard rubber. Day Lewis became Professor of Poetry at Oxford in 1951 and Poet Laureate in 1968.

A modern author of an entirely different genre was William Murray, who lived in Leckhampton for 40 years. He was the writer of the Ladybird books featuring Peter and Jane, considered an innovative reading scheme when introduced in the early 1960s. Murray was headmaster of

two Cheltenham schools catering for children with learning difficulties, Thirlestaine Court and Westlands, and he worked on the books with educational psychologist Joe McNally. The controlled vocabulary of the books was based on research that had identified the 200 words that make up nearly three-quarters of everyday reading matter. The books, featuring a white, middle-class, nuclear family, were considered out-dated by the 1990s, but Murray continued modernising the texts until his death in 1995.

A number of well-known writers, artists and musicians were actually born in Cheltenham or resident from an early age. Thomas Henry Sealy, a celebrated early Victorian writer and poet, was born in 1811 at Alstone Lawn, which was situated at the junction of Gloucester Road and Alstone Lane. His best-known works were *The Porcelain*

91　Alstone Lawn, 1820s, drawn and lithographed by Henry Lamb. Lamb was a drawing master in Cheltenham from c.1819-34 who published his own local views that were 'drawn from nature'. He owned a Fancy Repository in the High Street with a branch in the Long Room of the Old Well.

92 The warehouses and cellars of Dobell's, wine and spirit merchant, extended over two acres at the junction of Gloucester Road and Tewkesbury Road (now the site of Regent Components). In 1863 Dobell advertised himself as 'Sole agent for Her Majesty's Lochnagar Whiskey'.

Tower and a volume of poems entitled *The Old Man in the Wood*, and Cheltenham historian Goding likened his writings to those of Goldsmith and Lamb. As a young man Sealy travelled Europe before settling in Bristol where he founded the weekly *Great Western Advertiser*. Unfortunately this venture brought him financial ruin with estimated losses of £12,000, possibly contributing to his early death in 1848, aged 37. Although now largely forgotten, even in literary circles, Thomas Henry Sealy's name was still mentioned in Cheltenham guidebooks into the 1920s.

Poet Sydney Dobell began working as a clerk in his father's wine merchant's business in the Lower High Street at the age of 12. He was a bright boy, and a master of language, despite having never attended school or university, and his first work, 'The Roman', published in 1850, proved to be very popular. His poetry was praised by Tennyson and Dante Gabriel Rossetti. Dobell moved to many parts of Britain and Europe because of poor health, dying at Barton End near Painswick in 1874.

Adam Lindsay Gordon (1833-70) attended Cheltenham College for a year in 1841, and again in 1851. His father, formerly a Captain in the Bengal Cavalry, was Hindustani master at the College. Gordon was much involved in local sports and wrote the poem 'How we Beat the Favourite' after the 1847 Cheltenham Steeplechase. Unable to settle to a military career, he left for Australia in 1853 where he was considered the national poet and 'the best amateur steeplechase rider in the Colony'.

The poet James Elroy Flecker came to Cheltenham at the age of two, when his father was appointed first headmaster of Dean Close School in 1886. His earliest memories were of shopping in the Promenade with his mother, and the view of the Cotswolds from his nursery window. At the age of six he was sent to Miss Beale's mixed kindergarten, followed by attendance at Dean Close School, before going on to Trinity College, Oxford. After studying oriental languages at Caius College, Cambridge he joined the Diplomatic Service in 1906, serving as Vice-Consul in Beirut from 1911-13. Flecker was a prolific writer and many of his poems recalled his Cheltenham childhood. His health was always poor and he died of consumption in Switzerland in 1915 at the age of 30. His body was returned to Cheltenham for burial. A contemporary described his death as 'unquestionably the greatest premature loss that English literature has suffered since the death of Keats'.

Gustav Holst was born at 4 Clarence Road in 1874 and attended Cheltenham Grammar School where his father Adolph taught music. Adolph, an accomplished pianist, gave recitals at the Assembly Rooms and was organist at All Saints' Church. Gustav also showed an early aptitude for music and in 1892 he composed an operetta entitled *Lansdown Castle*, named after a crenellated building at the junction of Lansdown Road and Gloucester Road. The piece was enthusiastically

93 *Gustav Holst (left) with the Mayor of Cheltenham, Alderman Margrett, at the Holst Festival, held at the Town Hall in March 1927.*

received when first performed at Cheltenham Corn Exchange the following year, and Adolph was sufficiently impressed to borrow money to send his son to the Royal College of Music in London. Despite suffering from asthma and anaemia, Gustav regularly walked or cycled much of the way home to Cheltenham from the College. He wrote in a wide variety of musical styles, from songs for solo voice and chamber music to opera, ballet and massive orchestral works, taking his inspiration from many sources including Sanskrit and English folk song. In 1927 the Birmingham Orchestra performed Holst's works at a festival concert at Cheltenham Town Hall and despite ill health Holst himself conducted *The Planets*, his best-known work.

EIGHT

Theatre and Other Diversions

In Tudor times Cheltenham labourers were encouraged to develop useful skills such as archery and artillery practice, while laws regulated against games of chance and sports such as tennis and bowls. Large gatherings were discouraged for fear of spreading the plague, as recorded in the Manor Court book in 1611. Early that year Guy Dobbins had banged his drum through the town, advertising a play to be performed at the *Crown*, followed by numerous labourers, including one with a truncheon mimicking a marshallman. They refused to stop when ordered by the Bailiff, who was concerned about the plague at nearby Tredington and Prestbury, and were subsequently heavily fined.

Meetings, inquests and amusements were often held at inns and taverns, where sufficient accommodation was available. On 11 August 1741 the *Gloucester Journal* advertised a cudgel match opposite the *Plough*, with 'he that breaks the most heads in three bouts' to win a good hat and one guinea. A note added that 'betwixt the hours of 10 and 2, there will be a gown jigged for by the girls'. Bull-baiting with dogs was also advertised at this time, and cock-fighting remained popular into the 19th century. One local hero was the pugilist James 'Earywig' Edwards. Born in Rutland Street in 1822 Edwards became a local champion in the prize ring, and was acclaimed nationally as the 'king of the lightweights'. Edwards suffered a broken bone in his arm in the second round of a contest with Herbert 'the Mouse'; 167 rounds later nightfall ended the fight, which was declared a draw. On retiring from the ring Edwards became landlord of the *Roebuck Inn*, Lower High Street, but retained an interest in boxing, coaching Cheltenham College boys.

The first theatre building in Cheltenham was a converted malt house and stables in Coffee House Yard off Pittville Street. Despite the theatre's humble origins, Cheltenham audiences saw some of the most famous actors of the day. The Kemble family regularly performed there and John Kemble made his first appearance on that stage before establishing himself as a classical actor and theatrical manager. It was there too that the acting talents of his sister Sarah Siddons were recognised when she played Belvidera in *Venice Preserv'd* in 1774. David Garrick consequently invited her to perform at the Drury Lane Theatre, London. She went on to become one of the greatest English tragic actresses.

In 1779 John Boles Watson, who managed a group of touring players, 'The Cheltenham Company of Comedians', took over the running of the Coffee House Yard theatre, renamed the Theatre Royal following George III's visits. In 1805 Watson built a new Theatre Royal between Bath Street and the High Street. Supporters included Col Berkeley and Lord Byron, who arranged three benefits there for the famous clown Grimaldi. Sarah Siddons gave her final public performance at the Theatre Royal in 1812, in her greatest role, Lady Macbeth, before retiring to live with her brother John in North Street. Disaster struck in 1839 when fire destroyed the Theatre Royal and its contents. The Rev. Francis Close objected vehemently to all dramatic performances, and it was many years before another theatre was built. Plays were occasionally performed at the Assembly Rooms, and from 1849 onwards at Samuel Onley's new Music Hall on the site of the original Royal Well. It was not until 1891 that actress Lillie Langtry opened the New Theatre and Opera House in Regent Street. Built to a flamboyant design by Frank Matcham, architect of the London Palladium, the theatre flourished until after the Second World War. The increasing popularity of television reduced audience numbers, resulting in closure in 1959. Local people objected and within a year the theatre re-opened as the 'Everyman', today Gloucestershire's only professional theatre.

In the early 1800s Mr Seward and his touring marionette company often visited Cheltenham. In 1803 Seward set up a permanent puppet theatre at 27 St George's Place, which he named the Sadler's Wells Theatre, after the London theatre for which he had worked. The company performed every

94 A portrait of James Edwards (1822-57), 'Light Weight Champion of the World'. Standing to the right is another boxing champion, Tom Sayers, who came to live in Prestbury for a time. Both boxers sparred with the poet Adam Lindsay Gordon, who once knocked out Jem Edwards by a fluke.

95 Cheltenham Theatre and Opera House, 1927. Enormous crowds waiting to see the popular show 'No No Nanette', April 1927. The building's original frontage, which was unrecognisable in the 1960s, has now largely been restored to Matcham's original design.

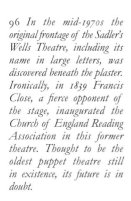

96 *In the mid-1970s the original frontage of the Sadler's Wells Theatre, including its name in large letters, was discovered beneath the plaster. Ironically, in 1839 Francis Close, a fierce opponent of the stage, inaugurated the Church of England Reading Association in this former theatre. Thought to be the oldest puppet theatre still in existence, its future is in doubt.*

night except Saturdays for nearly thirty years. After the deaths of Seward and his wife, Mr Belmont of the Theatre Royal re-opened the building as the New Clarence Theatre, and live actors replaced puppets. The venture was not a great success and in the 1830s the building became Gardner's Academy, a private seminary run by Joseph Aldan Gardner.

Harriot Mellon was considered one of the finest comic actresses of her time. Her mother Sarah and stepfather Thomas Entwisle had opened a High Street 'Musical Warehouse and Library' *c.*1802. When the position of Post-Master became vacant in 1805 it is thought that Harriot used her influence to secure the position for her stepfather, which he held until 1816. While performing in Cheltenham *c.*1810 Harriot Mellon met Thomas Coutts, a septuagenarian banker from London. Soon after being widowed in 1815, Harriot married Coutts, becoming the wife of the richest untitled commoner in England. After Coutts' death in 1822 Harriot married the Duke of St Albans, 20 years her junior. Despite her humble beginnings,

Harriot, Duchess of St Albans, was accepted by society. Cheltenham was also the birthplace of one of the leading Shakespearean actresses of the early 20th century, Lillah McCarthy, who was born in 1875 near the present Regent Arcade. George Bernard Shaw saw her perform as Lady Macbeth and became an ardent admirer and good friend. She went on to take the starring role in many of his plays, including that of Ann Whitefield in the first public performance of *Man and Superman* in 1905.

As balloon ascents became popular in the early 19th century, Cheltenham played host to many of the greatest aeronauts of the day. Thousands of people flocked to see James Sadler, a skilled veteran balloonist, who arrived in the town in September 1813. With no gas works in the town at that time, Sadler filled his balloon with hydrogen produced by mixing iron filings and sulphuric acid. Unfortunately, insufficient gas was produced to lift Sadler's own body weight, so his 17-year-old son Windham took his place in the balloon, which was launched from Alstone Wharf. Windham, who

ASCENT   AND   DESCENT

Mr Hampton's Balloon and Parachute, from the Montpellier Gardens, Cheltenham. October 3rd 1838.

97 *John Hampton's umbrella-like parachute, 15 feet in diameter and made of canvas, whalebone and bamboo, weighed about 200lb, including 56lb of ballast which was jettisoned just before landing to slow the final descent. Hampton was the first Englishman to make a successful parachute descent, and made six further jumps and over 100 balloon flights during his career.*

was on his first solo flight, encountered a heavy snowstorm at high altitude making it difficult to control the balloon, but he landed safely near Chipping Norton. Four years later he became the first person to cross the Irish Sea by balloon. Sadly he was killed in a balloon accident in 1824.

Charles Green, described as the greatest English aeronaut, visited Cheltenham in August 1822. After ascending from the *London Hotel* yard Green discovered that several lines on his balloon had been cut. He and his passenger were seriously injured when the balloon crash-landed close to Sapperton. Green later claimed that the balloon had been sabotaged because £20,000 had been wagered in London on the distance that he

would fly. Despite this incident Green returned to Cheltenham in April 1837 with his spectacular crimson and white striped Nassau balloon. This enormous 80ft high balloon had such tremendous lift that it needed over 2,000lb of weights and almost fifty people to hold it down. Green and his passengers ascended from Montpellier Gardens, ending their journey three hours later 90 miles away. In September 1838 aeronaut John Hampton announced that he would ascend in his balloon 'Albion' from Montpellier Gardens and return to earth using his 'improved Safety parachute'. On safety grounds the local magistrates only allowed him access to the town's gas supply if he agreed to tether the balloon. However, on reaching about

300 feet, Hampton severed the restraining ropes, and at 6,000 feet he cut loose his parachute. Spectators watched in horror as the balloon exploded, but Hampton escaped to land safely near Badgeworth over 12 minutes later.

Residents and visitors were treated to several exotic ventures in Cheltenham. Charles Hale Jessop established his Nursery Gardens in the 1820s supplying plants, seeds, bulbs and tools to the substantial private residences in the area. The Nursery soon extended over 20 acres of land behind St James' Square and Jessop was considered 'one of the first landscape gardeners of the day [with] extensive engagements in all parts of the kingdom and even on the continent'. Entry to the popular Gardens was free, and the grounds were described as 'a perfect picture of cultivated beauty', with ducks, owls, rabbits, fish and even a sea eagle as additional attractions. Disaster struck in 1855 when the river Chelt burst its banks, causing damage in excess of £800, nearly ten per cent of the entire estimated cost to the town. Recovery was slow and in 1858 Charles Jessop was declared bankrupt. His brother Jesse and son Josiah attempted to extend the zoological side of the business, adding Arctic foxes, armadillos, a heron, monkey house and maze. They charged 1d. entry, running the business virtually by themselves, but by 1872 the economic pressure had become too great and the Gardens closed. The site was used for railway expansion and light industry, then lay derelict for 40 years before commercial and residential development covered the area.

On 28 June 1838 the Gloucestershire Zoological, Botanical and Horticultural Gardens officially opened on 20 acres of land in Leckhampton. An

98 *Jessop's Nursery, 1826. Many visitors came to admire exotic plants, such as rice, bananas and breadfruit, which grew here. On 26 July 1855 tons of bricks, gravel, wood and mud were swept along by a raging torrent from the River Chelt that destroyed much of the nursery, submerging parts of the site under seven feet of floodwater.*

attractive lake in the shape of Africa was dug into the underlying clay and a second was planned in the shape of the Americas. Unfortunately this ambitious venture failed before completion and the architect Samuel Whitfield Daukes bought the property. In 1842 he re-opened it as public pleasure grounds known as Park Gardens, charging 1s. entrance fee. Even the attraction of matches at the newly opened Cheltenham and Gloucester Cricket Club in the grounds failed to save the Zoo, and in February 1844 the 'birds, beasts and

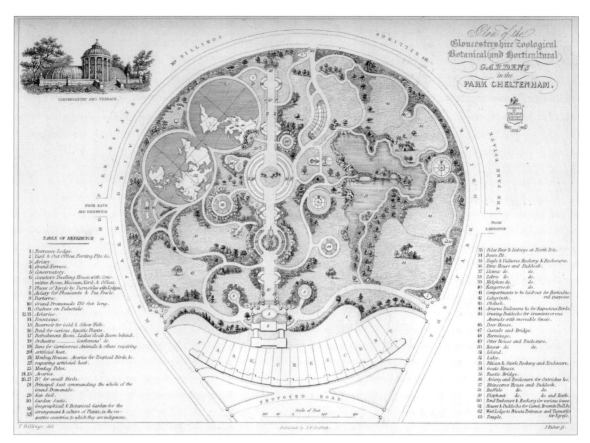

99 *The design for the Gloucestershire Zoological, Botanical and Horticultural Gardens in the Park, drawn by the owner, local solicitor Thomas Billings, shows the ambitious layout and range of attractions that he had planned. These included pelicans, monkeys, kangaroos and polar bears, a labyrinth, water cascade and an 'Elephant Walk'.*

reptiles' were auctioned at the Assembly Rooms. Much of the livestock, and a spectacular aviary in the form of a Chinese pagoda, were sold to Jessop's Gardens.

Montpellier Gardens were laid out as an ornamental pleasure ground for visitors to Montpellier Spa following its opening in 1809. They provided a fashionable promenade and a venue for public entertainment. In 1831 the Jearrad brothers, lessees of the Montpellier and Imperial Spas, erected an 'elegant and fanciful' Chinese pagoda opposite the Montpellier Spa. The celebrated Spa Band, resplendent in full military uniform, used the pagoda throughout the summer season. It was probably demolished after

the present bandstand was built in the Gardens in 1864.

There was constant rivalry between the Montpellier and Pittville spas, both providing a venue for public events such as flower shows, agricultural shows and exhibitions. One of the most spectacular events took place in 1866 at Pittville. A lifeboat, funded and equipped by the people of Cheltenham for the Royal National Lifeboat Institution, was brought to Cheltenham by train and paraded through the streets of the town before being launched on Pittville Lake in front of the Pump Room. The vessel was subsequently taken to Burnham-on-Sea where she became the first lifeboat to serve the busy shipping trade in the

Bristol Channel. A second, motorised lifeboat was launched on the lake in 1924 to raise funds for the RNLI in its centenary year, but the attendance of 2,000 was not enough to make a profit. In 1889, having previously been open only to subscribers, Pittville Pump Room and grounds were purchased by Cheltenham Borough Council and opened to the public as Pittville Park, with an extension to the west of Evesham Road. From 6-11 July 1908 Cheltenham staged the Gloucestershire Historical Pageant on and around the western lake. Marle Hill House was disguised as a medieval castle, and English historical scenes, from the Roman invasion to the 19th century, were re-enacted by about 3,000 people on the grass slope below it (now the golf course). On the far side of the lake 4,000 spectators watched from a specially constructed grandstand.

Liddington Lake Pleasure Gardens were opened near Leckhampton Station in 1893 on the site of flooded clay pits. The Gardens proved very popular, attracting visitors from miles around, at first on foot, and later by tram, to fish, swim, or to hire a canoe or rowing boat, and to ice-skate during the winter. Side shows, swings, slides, dances and concerts were also popular. The entrance fee included a trip around the central island aboard the *Pioneer* or *Mayflower* steam launches. One of the launches was transferred to Pittville Lake in 1910 where, on its first outing, the boat's boiler almost blew up because of over-enthusiastic stoking.

Many famous circus companies have performed in Cheltenham, including Hengler's, Newsome's and Barnum and Bailey's. The town had its own permanent circus building, which opened as Ryan's Equestrian Theatre in the grounds of Wellington Mansion, Bath Road in 1856. The Theatre, later known as Wellington Hall, specialised in breathtaking displays of horsemanship and acrobatics. The flimsy building burned down in

100 *The pagoda and 'Napoleon Fountain', Montpellier Gardens (1843). The Italian marble fountain was looted by the French in 1800, before being taken by the English. It was originally operated by a steam engine and could throw jets of water 32 feet into the air. The fountain is now displayed in the Broadwalk, Montpellier Spa Road.*

101 *Agricultural Show, Pittville, September 1867. This print and a review of the show were reported nationally in the* Illustrated London News.

102 *The first Cheltenham lifeboat was launched on Pittville Lake in October 1866, amidst the hearty and vociferous cheers of thousands, 'and the performance of Rule Britannia by the Bands of the Rifle Companies', according to the press. The self-righting vessel, which was 32 feet long with ten oars, remained in service at Burnham-on-Sea until 1887 and her crew saved 36 lives.*

103 Wellington Mansion, 1826. Named by its owner, Col Riddell, to celebrate the Duke of Wellington's stay in 1806. In 1816 Wellington planted an oak tree on the bank of the Chelt in the mansion grounds. Riddell later added the obelisk as a second memorial to Wellington.

1874, but was replaced by another on the same site. Also known as Ginnett's Hippodrome, and as the Colosseum, it was later taken over by the Salvation Army whose Citadel continues on the site today. Cheltenham was also the venue for one of the most spectacular shows ever seen in Britain when the legendary 'Buffalo Bill' Cody arrived by train with his 500 performers on 30 June 1903. His two shows probably took place on flat land adjacent to Prior's Road, each attracting more than 8,000 spectators. One of the performers was Fred Walters, known as 'the Blue Man', who had been educated at Cheltenham Grammar School.

In March 1865 American brothers William and Ira Davenport, successful stage spirit mediums, performed at the old Town Hall in Regent Street. Two respected local businessmen, James Lillywhite and John Smith Friskney, tied the seated Davenport brothers inside their wooden cabinet, the doors were closed and 'spiritual manifestations' began. Musical instruments were played and thrown through an aperture in the front of the cabinet and spirit hands mysteriously appeared, but when the doors were re-opened the two men were still securely tied. John Nevil Maskelyne, a watchmaker from Rotunda Terrace and a keen amateur illusionist, watched the performance closely throughout. In June 1865 Maskelyne, with his friend George Cooke, replicated the Davenports' entire performance in Jessop's Gardens 'in open daylight' but without spiritual aid. Cooke was a tailor, for a time in partnership with Elijah Shurmer in Winchcombe Street, and is said to have made the props for the illusions. The event was widely reported in the press, and Maskelyne and Cooke subsequently performed at the Crystal Palace in

104 *John Nevil Maskelyne (left), wife Elizabeth and their three children, all born in Cheltenham. Maskelyne founded a dynasty of three generations of illusionists, almost all of whom performed in Cheltenham. He is considered one of the fathers of modern magic.*

Paul on some of the earliest films and newsreels, including that of Queen Victoria's Diamond Jubilee procession in 1897. In 1896-7 Paul himself demonstrated his projector at the Ladies' College, in aid of the new Cricket Club ground, Hewlett Road. After Cooke's death in 1904, Maskelyne and Devant performed together at St George's Hall, London, until Maskelyne's death in 1917.

The first organised Cheltenham horse race took place on Nottingham Hill in 1815, but it was not until August 1818 that a more formal meet took place. This was arranged by Mr E. Jones of the *Shakespeare Inn*, Lower High Street, presumably to show off the prowess of his own horse, 'Tidmarsh', who won the mile-long flat race. In 1819 a three-mile course was opened on Cleeve Hill, with an impressive grandstand, visible from the Promenade. The first Gold Cup race, a flat race, took place that year with

1869 and before the Prince of Wales at Berkeley Castle in 1870.

From 1873 to 1903 Maskelyne and Cooke leased the Egyptian Hall, Piccadilly, later joined by another brilliant illusionist, David Devant. Early in 1896 Devant began showing 'animated photographs' at the Egyptian Hall, using one of the first film projectors in England, obtained from its inventor R.W. Paul. Devant toured the country with the new technology, visiting Cheltenham on several occasions. Maskelyne and Devant also worked with

a substantial prize of 100 guineas. The Races became an annual event, to the horror of Francis Close who railed against its evils. In 1829 mobs threw missiles at horses and riders and in 1830 the great grandstand mysteriously burned down. Undaunted, the organisers moved the event to Prestbury Park, where in 1834 the first steeplechase took place. From 1853 the event occupied various temporary sites, including the old Gloucester Road near Fiddler's Green, but returned permanently to Prestbury Park in 1898. Fred Archer, born near

105 *'Cryptical' winning the National Hunt Steeplechase on 14 March 1928. Watercolour by Nina Scott Langley, the renowned animal artist who lived in Cheltenham from 1920-36.*

106 *Cheltenham Archery Club Shoot, Montpellier Gardens, October 1910. Among the competitors was Cheltenham archer Queenie Newell, Olympic champion in 1908. The target bosses behind were almost certainly made at John Smith Friskney's sports depot at 23 Pittville Street, and were stored under Montpellier bandstand.*

107 *The Winter Gardens, 1922. Cheltenham's spectacular, though not always practical, venue for a wide variety of events between 1878-1940 housed one of the earliest roller-skating rinks in the country. The building dwarfed the new Town Hall, built in 1902-3, which gradually took on many of the entertainments.*

St George's Place in 1857, was one of racing's most successful jockeys. In 1858 his father became landlord of the *King's Arms* in Prestbury, and much of Fred's early training took place in and around the village. In 1868 he moved to Newmarket, becoming champion jockey of England at the age of 17. Sadly he suffered severe depression, caused by the death of his wife and son, financial difficulties and the constant battle to maintain his weight, and at the early age of 29 he shot himself.

The game of rugby football started at Rugby School *c.*1823, and by the middle of the century it had spread to Oxford and Cambridge Universities, and to public schools across the country, including Cheltenham College. However, it was not until 1886 that a standard set of rules was adopted nationally, and this included the principle known as the 'Cheltenham College rating'. The rating, which had been in force at the College for about 20 years, equated three tries to one goal. The

108 *Gloucestershire Cricket Club, Cheltenham College, August 1894. Captained by W.G. Grace (seated third right) the team also included his brother Dr E.M. Grace (seated fourth left) and G.L. Jessop (seated second left). Born in Cambray Place, Jessop became known as 'The Croucher' and succeeded W.G. Grace as captain in 1898.*

modern scoring values were not adopted until 1905, the same year that the New Zealand All Blacks toured Great Britain for the first time. On 6 December that year 8,000 spectators watched Cheltenham Rugby Football Club play the All Blacks at Cheltenham Athletic Ground. The home team lost 18-0, but the visitors were full of praise for the way their hosts had played.

In the mid-19th century archery was considered an acceptable pastime for women as well as men. Cheltenham Archery Club was established in 1856, meeting in Montpellier Gardens. It became one of the foremost English archery societies, thanks largely to its founder, Horace Alfred Ford, said to have been the greatest target archer of all time, winning the national title on 12 occasions. He was instrumental in turning a fashionable amusement into a serious sport, by applying scientific principles. Cheltenham boasted some of the best women archers in the country. Alice Blanche Legh was Champion Archer of Great Britain an astonishing 23 times from 1881-1922, while her sister Beata Mary rarely missed winning a medal in 53 years of National Competition from 1885-1938.

Croquet was another activity in which women were allowed to participate, and in the 1860s some of the game's most influential promoters were from the Cheltenham area. After a lapse of interest in favour of tennis, the game found renewed popularity in the late 19th century, with a tournament held at the East Gloucestershire Club in 1898. The founding of the present Cheltenham Croquet Club followed in 1904, and in 1920 it purchased the land for the present courts beside the Old Bath Road for £800. The Club has hosted the British National Championships every year (except 1983) since 1972, and has been one of the principal venues for international matches.

Twins Willie and Ernest Renshaw dramatically increased the popularity of British lawn tennis in the 1880s with their exciting, competitive play. In the early 1870s the twins lived with their mother and stepfather Edward Meara, a retired naval captain, at Clarence House, Imperial Square, and attended Cheltenham College as dayboys. The brothers were both rivals and accomplices, winning 13 Wimbledon titles separately and as doubles partners between 1881 and 1889. Their domination of the game was so complete that the period became known as the 'Renshaw Rush'. Willie's record for the shortest-ever men's singles final has never been bettered – it took him just 37 minutes to beat John Hartley in 1881.

In 1872 James Lillywhite, popular cricket coach at Cheltenham College for 17 years, proposed that a county match should be played there in the summer holidays. W.G. Grace captained the Gloucestershire side which beat Surrey by an innings. This match established an annual event, organised by Lillywhite until the year before his death in 1882. In August 1878 he was paid £120 to organise two successive county matches on the grounds. A 'pronounced social success', the event became known as Cricket Week, and then was renamed Cheltenham Cricket Festival in 1906 when three county matches were played on the College grounds for the first time. 'Jem' Lillywhite, a member of the famous cricketing family, ran a sports shop in Cheltenham from 1862-82, supplied by the family sports manufactory in south-east London. He was also one of the first managers of the Winter Gardens, ran a 'velocipede school' at the old Town Hall in Regent Street in 1870, and was co-lessee of the Montpellier Rotunda and Gardens. The proceeds from the first Cricket Festival were given to Jem Lillywhite's widow, Eliza.

NINE

Improvement and Innovation

Cheltenham was extremely isolated until the end of the 18th century, due mainly to the appalling state of the surrounding roads. Even the road to Gloucester was often impassable and in 1513 William Greville of Arle left money for its repair in his will. Richard Pate, in his charitable endowments to the town, requested that any surplus should be used to repair the Gloucester road. Eventually, in the 1780s the Gloucester-Cheltenham turnpike was built, using harder Bristol stone to supplement local supplies from Churchdown Hill and Cooper's Hill. Other main roads around Cheltenham were turnpiked between 1785 and 1825 and new roads built to major towns. An advertisement of 1738 reveals that Cheltenham passengers had to travel to Andoversford to catch the London coach, the *Gloucester Flying Machine*, which boasted a 'short' three-day journey. A direct Cheltenham-London coach was not available until *c*.1770.

Commercial traffic improved with the opening of the Coombe Hill Canal in 1796-7, enabling coal and building supplies to be brought nearer to the town from the River Severn. In June 1811 a horse-drawn tramway was opened along the new Gloucester Road, running from Alstone Wharf to Gloucester Docks, with a branch line along Queens Road to the Leckhampton quarries. In 1831 this route was used for public transport when a steam road carriage, designed by Sir Goldsworthy Gurney, provided a Gloucester-Cheltenham service. The steam coaches made four round-trips daily, and in

the course of the project travelled 4,000 miles and carried some 3,000 passengers. It was abandoned after only four months as there was considerable local opposition and the noisy equipment damaged the roadway. The earlier horse-drawn tramway was rendered obsolete when the Birmingham & Gloucester (later Midland) Railway arrived in Cheltenham, with the opening of Lansdown Station in June 1840. This was followed seven years later by the Great Western Railway station at St James' Square, built on part of Jessop's Gardens.

Public transport within the town was limited to two sedan chairs in 1781, available for hire at 6d. per trip. Gradually wheelchairs and flys were introduced, then a larger fleet of hackney carriages. In June 1890 the Cheltenham Omnibus Company's first horse-drawn omnibus ran between Lansdown Station and Pittville Gates. This short-lived venture was replaced when the Cheltenham & District Light Railway Company began an electric tram service between Lansdown and Cleeve Hill in August 1901. Motor buses were introduced in 1912 and finally replaced the electric trams in 1930-1. An echo of the trams occurred in the late 1990s when three gas-powered road trains, the Spa Shuttles, provided free transport around the town centre. Nicknamed 'Noddy-trains', and with annual running costs of £250,000, they were withdrawn in September 1999.

The local influence of the manor declined from the 16th century and gradually the Parish

109 *Steam train, Lansdown Station, 1862. Samuel Whitfield Daukes designed the station with an imposing Doric portico that was regrettably removed in 1961.*

Vestry assumed more responsibility for running the town. Its authority was shown to be limited, however, as the spa town developed during the 18th century. The reluctance of Cheltenham inhabitants to acknowledge the new spa status was reported in the *Morning Post* of 6 September 1780: 'They seem displeased that chance should ever have brought them to public notice, by their constant opposition to every improvement for the convenience and accommodation of those who visit them.' An Act of Parliament of 1786 appointed a body of Town Commissioners to raise a rate for paving, cleansing and lighting the town. At first improvements were limited, judging from the Rev. T.D. Fosbroke's description of the open drains at the lower end of the High Street in 1798: 'an inconvenience which rendered the path utterly unfit for gossiping or thoughtful promenade, because absence or occupation of the mind occasioned a fall into them'. Subsequent Acts of 1806, 1821 and 1852 increased the Commissioners' powers, giving greater responsibility for public services. The Borough Council replaced the Town Commissioners in 1876.

In 1560 the Manor Court ordered the miller, Richard Pate, to deflect the water from the Cambray millpond once a week, to flow down the High Street 'according to ancient custom'. However, this centuries-old method of cleaning the High Street had become a hindrance by the time of the 1786 Act. Over the centuries the mill owners had proved reluctant to allow a sufficient flow of water. The Commissioners diverted the Chelt from the centre of the High Street to run along channels either

110 *One of the last Cheltenham wheelchairmen, Mr Alfred Coveney, photographed in the 1920s with a lady patron who was over 100 at the time.*

111 *Laying tramway extensions in the High Street in 1905. The tramlines were set in wooden paving blocks supplied by the Acme Flooring & Paving Co. After heavy rain some of the blocks would swell and pop up out of the road causing considerable consternation to road users.*

112 *One of Cheltenham's short-lived transport ventures was the introduction of rickshaws in October 1910. The proprietors of the scheme were Mr and Mrs Alexander Clifton, seen here as passengers in two of the rickshaws.*

113 *The opening of the public abattoir, Gloucester Road, led to the closure of numerous private slaughterhouses in the town, although many were still operating in the early part of the 20th century.*

114 *An early advertisement for water closets, 1818. Mr Gore's premises were in St George's Place, where Cheltenham's first public sewer ran under the street to empty into the Chelt.*

Cheltenham Examiner correspondent complained about animals roaming the streets, having been attacked by a bull in the London Road. The last animal-processing nuisance was removed from Cheltenham with the closure of a skin merchant company at Lower Alstone House in the 1970s.

In 1806 Dr Edward Jenner sought permission to open a drain from his house to join Cheltenham's first public sewer, in St George's Place. Jenner was one of the Town Commissioners, but is only recorded speaking at the meetings on two occasions, both regarding sewers. In 1808 he proposed building a sewerage system to serve the whole town, but only one sewer was made, running down Old Well Lane from Montpellier to the Chelt. In the 1820s the architect Papworth was paid £52 to prepare estimates and take levels for a common sewer under the High Street, but it was not until 1833 that the Cheltenham Sewers Company was formed. During the 19th century life became increasingly uncomfortable for millers working with fouled watercourses. The Commissioners bought the Sewers Company in 1857 and in 1870 the Hayden Sewage Farm was officially inaugurated, replacing the outfall of Cheltenham's sewage near Lower Alstone Mill. Despite this, complaints about effluent in Cheltenham watercourses continued until the end of the century. In August 1900 the foul odour from Hayden Sewage Farm was so strong that surprise was expressed that any man who worked there was still alive.

side of the newly-made road, but the arguments continued while they still claimed access to the water from the millpond. The old stepping stones across the High Street were revealed when a sewer was being laid in 1834.

The Commissioners also attempted to regulate the nuisance of piggeries and slaughterhouses, present in almost every street, and animal fairs that were held in a variety of locations. Horses were traditionally sold at the junction of Albion Street and Winchcombe Street, pigs in the Fleece yard beside Gardner's Brewery, and horned cattle and sheep near Henrietta Street. In 1876 a purpose-built market opened on the site of the demolished Albion Brewery, Gloucester Road. In spite of this there were still 40 abattoirs in the town, and debate continued as to whether pigs should be kept within 30 yards of any dwelling. In May 1876 a stray cow belonging to Mr Page, a High Street butcher, escaped while being herded along Lansdown from Gloucester. It chased two Misses Perry into Waite & Kite, a chemist at the top of Montpellier, and demolished the counters and displays. It trampled on one Miss Perry, tearing off her left ear, before running out to rejoin the herd. As late as 1891 a

The supply of clean water for Cheltenham often caused concern. A private company was formed in 1824, providing piped water to those willing to pay, from the first of five reservoirs at the Hewletts. Prior to this Cheltenham had depended on private wells and rainwater tanks. There were frequent complaints that the Water Company provided an inadequate and intermittent supply, until eventually a Bill passed in 1878 allowed Cheltenham Corporation to acquire the waterworks. In October 1886 Dowdeswell Reservoir was opened, lowering the River Chelt by about 20 feet and reducing the flood risk to Cheltenham. Disastrous floods had occurred during the previous 100 years, ruining property, especially in the Promenade. These floodwaters stretched for hundreds of yards either side of the Chelt by the time they reached Alstone, destroying the produce in the market gardens.

Lighting the town began in 1787 with 120 oil lamps placed along the High Street, lit only in the autumn and winter months. The Cheltenham Gas Manufactory was established on the Tewkesbury Road c.1815 and in 1818 the site expanded to become the Cheltenham Gas, Light and Coke Co., one of the earliest gas-lighting ventures in England. On 29 September that year the first gas lamps were lit in the High Street. In 1852 Cheltenham was said to be one of the best lit towns in the country with 786 gaslights along the streets. Electricity first arrived with a private installation at the Central Iron Works, Lansdown, in 1882. Electricity for the town was introduced in 1894, with the building of a central electricity station in Arle Road, and the first electric street lamps were officially switched on in February 1897.

One building demolished during improvements was the town lock-up behind the old Booth Hall. Known as the Blind House, it was a round, stone,

115 *Waterfall at the end of Pittville boating lake with the edge of a mill building on the right, 1901. In 1851, when Mr Stratford ran the mill, Wyman's Brook, on which it stands, was effectively the sewer for the Pittville district and much of Prestbury.*

116 *Neptune's Fountain, c.1900, designed by the Borough Engineer Joseph Hall, with the relocated Sherborne Spa building in the background. The fountain is fed by the Chelt, which runs beneath. Hall also designed the unusual redbrick electricity offices on the corner of Clarence Street and St George's Place.*

two-roomed building with the words 'Do well and fear not' carved on the wall and a set of stocks alongside. Other instruments of punishment were a whipping-post in Alstone Lane and a gallows in the Marsh area (St Paul's). The latter was used in 1777 to hang a dishonest footman who had murdered his mistress, Mrs A'Court, during a visit to Cheltenham. The Blind House was replaced in 1788 with a small lock-up in Fleece Lane, then a larger gaol on the corner of New Street, used from 1813-40. A County Police Force, established by the County Magistrates in 1840, replaced an earlier police force created by the Commissioners. Cheltenham was one of the County Police headquarters, with a station initially in St George's Place. From 1858 until 1970 the station occupied

the former *Clarence Hotel* in Crescent Place, before moving to Lansdown Road.

After the formation of the Town Commissioners the Parish Vestry retained responsibility for the poor. The prosperity of the town had fluctuated, perhaps the lowest point being in 1441 when an Act was passed releasing the inhabitants from taxes 'on account of the poverty of the place'. A Church House existed at the Chester Walk entrance to the parish churchyard, accommodating four poor inhabitants and supported by charitable donations. When demolished by the Vestry in 1813 a date of 1507 was discovered carved above the door. The Vestry leased various properties to house the poor until 1808-9 when a parish workhouse was built near the Knapp, behind St James' Square. The

Vestry ran this until 1834 when responsibility was transferred to a Poor Law Union, administered by a Board of Guardians and covering 12 parishes. A large Union Workhouse was opened in Swindon Road in 1841 housing 581 inmates.

One solution to poverty in the town during the latter half of the 19th century was the emigration of poor children to Canada. This was strongly supported in Cheltenham, but large numbers still remained. During a severe frost in January 1879 a Committee for the Relief of the Unemployed Poor provided bread and coal to 1,700 and gave employment to an average of 150 men daily. Many of these lived in the narrow crowded streets off the Lower High Street and Tewkesbury Road. As late as 1902 Josephine Butler, the pioneering social reformer, wrote of Cheltenham, 'There are low class brothels and slums which would be a disgrace to London or New York'. She had lived in Cheltenham from 1857-66, during her husband's employment as Vice Principal of Cheltenham College. In 1864, while living at the Priory, their five-year-old daughter Eva died in a fall, which tragic event made Josephine determined to help those who suffered 'pain greater than mine own'.

Private benefactors also provided for the Cheltenham poor, the most notable being Richard Pate. In 1578 he founded an Almshouse for six elderly poor, to include two women, situated on the High Street, opposite Rodney Road. It had a chapel attached, an orchard and a patch of garden for each inmate, who received a small weekly income and enough black cloth for gowns. In 1811 the Fellows

117 *The Union Workhouse, Swindon Road, 1978. Designed as a central irregular hexagon, with radiating wings accommodating the sexes separately, the site included a chapel and a stone-breaking yard. It became St Paul's Hospital from 1948-97 and most of the buildings were gradually replaced. St Paul's Medical Centre now occupies the site. (Photograph by Steven Blake.)*

118 *The Elms (site of Pope's Close), seat of the Ricketts family, was purchased by the Board of Guardians in 1882 to accommodate the workhouse children.*

119 *The Bucklehaven Almshouses, Charlton Kings, newly built in 1911. In his will John Charles Buckle provided for these homes for deserving aged and infirm men and women in reduced circumstances. The original intention of forming a quadrangle was not carried out, although another line of almshouses was added in 1997 at right angles to this one, making 26 units in all.*

of Corpus Christi College, Oxford, managers of the Pate Foundation, exchanged the property with Thomas Smith, a banker, for the inferior site of the present Almshouse in Albion Street, without chapel or orchard. Smith paid £250 on gaining the larger site, and once the inmates had left he sold it for £2,000; the *Vittoria Hotel* was built there soon afterwards. The Hay Memorial Cottage Homes opened in July 1894 in Naunton Park, provided by John Alexander Hay and his wife for the aged and deserving poor. In 1911 the Bucklehaven Almshouses, for impoverished gentlewomen, opened in Charlton Kings, the gift of John Charles Buckle, of Redland, Bristol, who died in 1899. The Jesse Mary Chambers Almshouses were established in July 1924 in Tennyson Road by a Reading gentleman in memory of his sister. Dowty House in St Margaret's Road, formerly a boys' orphanage, opened in 1958 as a home for

37 elderly, largely thanks to George Dowty who encouraged contributions from his workforce and himself donated £2,000 instead of buying a new Rolls Royce.

In 1806 Mrs Williams of Prestbury founded a Female Orphan Asylum and School of Industry for girls. It opened in a converted thatched barn in a lane off the upper High Street and Queen Charlotte became its patron in the early years. The day's work consisted almost entirely of housework, with an hour's reading and spelling practice every evening, and religious worship and instruction at each end of the day. In 1818 the asylum moved to Winchcombe Street and in 1823 occupied a new building, re-built in 1834. This last building, known as Charlotte House, remained in use until 1958 when it was demolished following closure.

Private benefactors also supplied public drinking fountains for the poor in Victorian

120 *The upper part of Winchcombe Street, 1840s, looking towards Pittville Gates with Charlotte House, the Female Orphan Asylum, on the right.*

121 *The earliest public drinking fountain, Lower High Street, 1903. The fountain was designed by the Borough Engineer Henry Dangerfield in 1860, as was a second fountain situated at the rear of the Market Place.*

Cheltenham. The first was erected in March 1860 at the High Street end of White Hart Row. A second was established at the rear of the Market Place later that year, financed by Miss Carrington. Within a few years they were considered a great nuisance, and the Market Place fountain was transported to Crystal Palace in 1868. In 1871 Miss Elizabeth Baillie of Tivoli offered to erect a drinking fountain in the open space at the present Gordon Lamp. However, the Town Commissioners proposed replacing a cab stand in Clarence Street with her fountain. The resulting dispute with the cab drivers evidently exasperated Miss Baillie, who donated

£110 to the hospital instead. In 1891 a drinking fountain was placed at Westal Green, donated by the three Misses Whish to celebrate their 50 years' residence. It was designed by the sculptor A.B. Wall, and in 1929 was moved to its present site in Sandford Park (Keynsham Road).

The provision of health services for the townspeople began with the opening of the Cheltenham Medical Dispensary in Winchcombe Street in 1813. By 1832, having moved to 318 High Street, fund-raising had begun to replace the Dispensary and Casualty Hospital with a General Hospital. In April 1834 the *Cheltenham Chronicle* reported that nearly £6,000 had been raised, but commented on a subscription from Signor Pedrotti, Professor of Italian and Guitar: 'We trust his generous example will be followed by other professors … who owe much, perhaps *all* of their wealth and respectability, to English liberality.' In 1837 the first General Hospital and Dispensary opened at Segrave House (later Idmiston House, now Normandy House) in the Lower High Street. In 1839 the tower extension was added, providing wards for 40 patients and operating theatres on the attic floor. R.W. Jearrad designed this extension and the frontage, providing the plans and his time without charge. Evidently interested in public welfare, Jearrad invented a washing-machine in 1849. It was successfully trialled in the St George's Workhouse, Hanover Square, London, and proved excellent for sterilising the clothing of those affected by cholera and other contagious diseases. It was also economic and could wash six dozen towels in just four minutes. In 1849 the present General Hospital, designed by D.J. Humphris, opened in Sandford Road and was considered a model hospital building at that time.

Other health provision in the town included a Homoeopathic Dispensary, established in Rodney Terrace in 1856, and an Ophthalmic

122 *Segrave House (now Normandy House), 1840s. Built as a private house in 1813, it was bought from Robert Capper, president of the hospital board, and altered and extended by R.W. Jearrad in 1839 to accommodate the General Hospital and Dispensary.*

Infirmary at Bournemouth House, St George's Place, in operation from 1861-82. Miss Susan Delancey bequeathed £5,000 in 1866 towards the establishment of a town fever hospital. This opened in 1874 as the Delancey Fever Hospital in Charlton Lane, designed by John Middleton. Dr F.A. Smith founded an Ear, Eye & Throat Infirmary in North Place in 1889, which received patients from as far afield as Monmouth and Malmesbury. Health care expanded during the 20th century, and in 1908 School Medical Inspections were started in Cheltenham. The first annual report stated that some parents had objected to having their children 'tampered with', 'exposed' or 'assaulted'. 'No notice was taken of these objectors, and I believe that will be the shortest way of dealing with them'; not a response that would be tolerated today.

Cheltenham had no full-time fire brigade until 1813, when an insurance company provided a service for private subscribers only. In 1615, when malt houses presented a considerable fire risk, each maltster had to provide a leather bucket, and the townspeople were taxed to pay for a ladder. A

sanctus bell in the parish church tower was once used as a fire-bell, and a fire engine and buckets were kept in the north porch entrance. A tablet opposite the rose window records that Sir John Dutton presented a fire engine to the town in 1721, as did Lord Gage in the 1730s. Eventually the Town Commissioners paid an insurance company to supply a fire service for the whole town, for a time provided from Wellington Passage by the Phoenix Insurance Company. A fire engine was kept near the Chelt in Rodney Road, then called Engine House Lane. In 1906 the Fire Station was opened in St James' Square and the fire brigade moved to the present Keynsham Road headquarters in 1959. One long-serving fireman was Samuel John Such, who captained the brigade for 21 years from 1894. He was also a general smith, art metal worker, coppersmith, wheelwright, pattern maker, hot water engineer, draughtsman, mechanical engineer, inventor and patentee, millwright and founder of the Caledonian Works in King Street.

Other local inventors included Isaac James of the Tivoli Works, who won a prize at the Royal

123 *The Fire Brigade proudly pose in front of the new Fire Station, St James' Square, 1906. Two years earlier Mrs Percy Theobald had presented the town with the Merryweather steam fire engine on the left.*

Agricultural Show in July 1857 for his liquid manure distributor. In July 1873 a new and patented improvement in butchers' carts was produced at Messrs Dredge Carriage Works, Bath Road. It was invented by Capt. J.E. Acklam and 'applied the refrigerating power of moist felt and zinc' to the chamber that carried the meat. Two Central Iron Works employees, engineering manager Leonard Mansfield and chief draughtsman Robert C. Puckering, won a prize of 100 guineas in October 1884 for their designs for machinery to make patent fuel out of coal slack. William John Stephenson-Peach, Instructor in Civil Engineering at Cheltenham College from 1892-1900, is credited

with inventing the first mains electric lawnmower, applying for patents in March 1895 and August 1896. He went on to teach at Malvern College and it was in his engineering workshops there that much of the machining work for the first Morgan motor car was carried out by H.F.S. Morgan.

Perhaps the man whose innovation created the most far-reaching improvement was Dr Edward Jenner, the pioneer of smallpox vaccination. In 1795 he and his family occupied lodgings opposite a druggist's shop in the Lower High Street, but moved into 8 St George's Place (now 22) the following year, to live there on a seasonal basis. At Alpha House (St George's Road) Jenner offered free vaccinations to the poor during a smallpox outbreak in 1800. Called 'the pest house' by the locals, Alpha House was a farmhouse belonging to surgeon, Thomas Cother. In 1809, in response to the anti-vaccinists, Jenner retorted that he had successfully vaccinated 3-4,000 people in the Cheltenham area during a smallpox epidemic. He always preferred his home town of Berkeley but he did recommend Cheltenham in a letter to Miss Wait, a Bristol patient. He even suggested she try the wide variety of spa waters, adding with characteristic dry wit, 'to this I attach no more value than that which flows from my Tea Kettle'. Following his wife's death in 1815 Jenner rarely visited Cheltenham, choosing to live permanently in Berkeley.

124 *Edward Jenner, part of Cheltenham College Chapel reredos, carved by R.L. Boulton & Sons, 1904. The only other memorials to Cheltenham's most illustrious resident are the street name Jenner Walk, a Civic Society blue plaque on Jenner's St George's Place home (rebuilt), and a plaque on Alpha House, St George's Road, which incorrectly states that Jenner once lived there.*

TEN

Working Lives

Cheltenham's economy was largely dependent on agriculture, malting and the market for centuries, but other trades helped to make the town self-supporting. John Smyth's *Men and Armour* shows the range of occupations in the Cheltenham Hundred in 1608. Not surprisingly, of the 351 men listed, 128 were engaged in agriculture. The others included 13 shoemakers, 13 tailors, 12 weavers, 12 maltsters, eight carpenters, six butchers, six tanners, four bakers, one chandler, one smith, one scrivener, one wheelwright and one cooper. In addition there were 28 servants, some of whom would have been involved in agriculture. The large number of tailors and shoemakers supplied customers attending the market from as far afield as Andoversford and

Southam. The parish register entries of the early 17th century reveal that almost all the tanners mentioned were from Alstone, suggesting a well-established tanning industry there.

In the 1690s John Prinn, the Manor Steward, wrote of Cheltenham that 'its soil is sandy and very naturale for carrets, cabbages, and turnips, insomuch that the whole neighbourhood for sundry miles around is annually furnished with these three from this towne'. Market gardening remained a feature of Alstone, Charlton Kings and Leckhampton until well into the 20th century, and opportunities were created for domestic gardeners as the number of large private residences increased. The first Cheltenham Horticultural Society was established in 1825, introducing a competitive element to gardening, and glasshouses provided exotic fare for the tables of the gentry. In 1868 James Cypher established the five-acre Cypher's Exotic Nurseries in Queens Road, which exported flowers and plants all over the world. In 1902 Cypher's Nurseries were awarded gold and silver medals by the Royal Horticultural Society for their orchids. The business closed in 1960.

125 *The workforce of Messrs James Cypher & Sons of Queen's Road Nurseries in 1907 with a consignment of orchids bound for Japan. This was one of many such orders for a rich Japanese baron and consisted of nearly 1,000 plants, which travelled via Canada.*

Almost all the mills along the Chelt were corn mills. However,

126 *A Victorian vinery attached to Stratford House, Suffolk Square. Exotic plants and flowers for private glasshouses were obtainable locally from many of Cheltenham's nurserymen. Stratford House was probably named by one of its residents, Captain Shakespear, RN.*

there were references during Henry V's reign to a fulling mill at Cudnall in Charlton Kings, let to Robert and Joan Walker, suggesting that Cheltenham had some involvement in the cloth industry. Bedlam Mill at Swindon village was a cloth mill by 1775, and a nearby field, Mill Platt, was renamed Rack Close after the method of drying cloth on racks. A number of weavers in Cheltenham are mentioned in the Manor Court rolls; there were at least nine weavers in 1417, and a tucker and a silk weaver in 1608. The invention of the flying-shuttle, patented in 1733, meant an increase in the speed of weaving, and a consequent shortage of spinners to prepare the additional yarn required. The *Cheltenham Guide* of 1781 mentioned that many of the town's women and children spun woollen yarn for the Stroud clothiers. The *Guide*

also noted the town's white cotton stockings 'which for fineness, texture and value vie with those of most towns'. As late as 1827 Thomas Baker is recorded, in the King Street Ebenezer Chapel registers, as being a teazle-grower from the Golden Valley on the outskirts of Cheltenham.

Tobacco was introduced into the Cheltenham area in 1619 when the Crown granted monopoly privileges to individuals who founded new enterprises. These created employment for the labouring poor and generated income for the gentlemen developers. One such entrepreneur was John Stratford, of Prestbury and London, who leased pieces of land from different owners to make up an initial tobacco crop of 100 acres. The other owners were the wife of Timothy Gates, parson, with land in Bishops Cleeve, Thomas Loreng of

127 Arle Court, c.1860, one of the seats of the Lygon family who let 12 acres of land in the area in 1619 for part of the first tobacco crop grown in this country. (Photograph courtesy of the Bristol and Gloucestershire Archaeological Society.)

armed multitude and obstructive local magistrates greeted them. Beaman retreated to Gloucester reporting that, 'Abundance of tobacco there is about Cheltenham, and very good. I think that ten men cannot destroy it in four days.' Local cultivation continued and in 1675 Ogilby wrote that Winchcombe and Cheltenham were populated by a people 'much given to plant tobacco, though they are supprest by authority'. Eventually the fall in the price of Virginia tobacco made it unprofitable to risk planting the illicit crop. However, as late as 1691 a Cheltenham miller, Richard Teale, demanded compensation from the government following the destruction of a small field of tobacco that he had planted 'in ignorance of the law'.

Haymes in Bishops Cleeve, Sir John Tracy of Toddington, Giles Broadway of Postlip, and John Ligon, Esq., who let 12 acres of his land at Arle Court. It was a short-lived venture, however, as the government banned tobacco growing in England at the end of that same year, in order to improve the prospects of Virginia growers. Although John Stratford promptly ceased his operations, the year's work had been enough to teach the local population how to cultivate tobacco, which they continued to do for another 70 years.

In 1634 William King, sent by the Privy Council to destroy the tobacco crops, reported that there were considerable quantities being grown in Winchcombe, Cheltenham, Tewkesbury, Gotherington, Arle and Charlton Kings. An Act passed in 1652 prohibiting the planting of tobacco in England was met with a petition from the local growers, who were then permitted to keep the crop planted 'for this year only'. The same concession was granted the following year. Growers defended their crops fiercely, and when a troop of 36 horse, led by John Beaman, was sent in 1658 to destroy the tobacco of Winchcombe and Cheltenham, an

Robert Atkyns described Cheltenham in 1712 as 'a town considerably engaged in the Malt trade', the barley for this being grown in the town's common fields. Brewing had been important to the town and its market for centuries. In 1527 there were 12 licensed brewers in the town, including George Hurst, who lived at the courthouse, and a woman, Joanna Chesenall. There were two innkeepers, Henry Corston and Walter Pate, and the price of new best beer was set at 2½d. per gallon. Rate books of the early 1700s showed that a quarter of all buildings in the town were malt houses. Cider and perry making were prevalent throughout the Severn Vale and an Act of 1763 imposing an excise duty on cider proved extremely unpopular in Cheltenham. The Act was passed to raise revenue following war with France, but in Cheltenham the proclamation of peace was read by a youth dressed in mourning, reflecting the town's disgust at the cider tax. In the 1920s Charlton Kings alone still had six operational cider mills.

In 1760 John Gardner and a Mr Leversage from Middle Lypiatt founded Gardner's Brewery, later the Original Brewery, in Fleece Lane (Henrietta Street). This was an ideal site as it contained a well that was 35 feet in depth, yielding 27,000 gallons of water a day. There were a number of smaller breweries in the town including the Albion Brewery, established on the new Gloucester Road c.1820. The Cheltenham Original Brewery Company gradually absorbed its local rivals, including the Cheltenham Steam Brewery in 1897. In 1959 the Cheltenham and the Stroud breweries were amalgamated to form West Country Brewery Holdings Ltd. Whitbread acquired this in 1963 and the brewery continued to expand in the area north of the High Street, building a seven-storey headquarters in Monson Avenue. On 1 October 1998 brewing came to an end in Cheltenham with the closure of the 250-year-old brewery. The name of Malthouse Lane in St Paul's, where James Agg-Gardner had a malt house for the Cheltenham Original Brewery, serves as a reminder.

In the 16th century Cheltenham's market consisted of a Market Hall and Booth Hall, which was used as a second market, a High Cross (near the present Promenade entrance) and a town lock-up. In 1654 Christopher Bayley, the master of the Grammar School, left £80 in his will to rebuild one of the market houses which had become dilapidated. Its replacement was a freestanding, pillared structure with a room above for use as a wool market and for holding court leets, sited in the centre of the High Street opposite the *Plough*. Known as the Corn Market and Butter Cross, it survived until demolition by the Town Commissioners in 1786. John Everis and Thomas Keyte were employed to build a new market house, almost opposite North Street. A second Market Hall was built next to it in 1808, the older one being used for the sale of earthenware and glass until its collapse in 1811. The 1808 Market House, with an upper room designated as the Town Hall, also became too small for the increasing volume of trade. It was altered and refronted in 1823 for

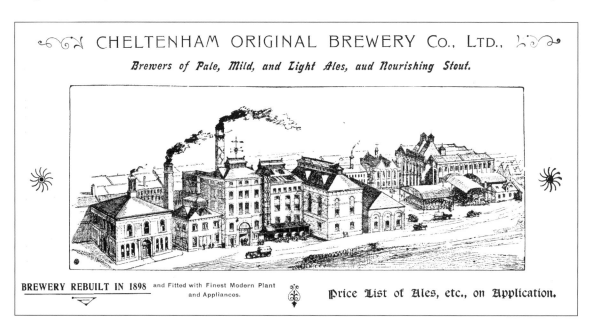

CHELTENHAM ORIGINAL BREWERY Co., Ltd.,

Brewers of Pale, Mild, and Light Ales, and Nourishing Stout.

BREWERY REBUILT IN 1898 and Fitted with Finest Modern Plant and Appliances.

Price List of Ales, etc., on Application.

128 *The Cheltenham Original Brewery Co. Ltd, 1901, from the east. The brewery had been extensively rebuilt in 1898 following a disastrous fire.*

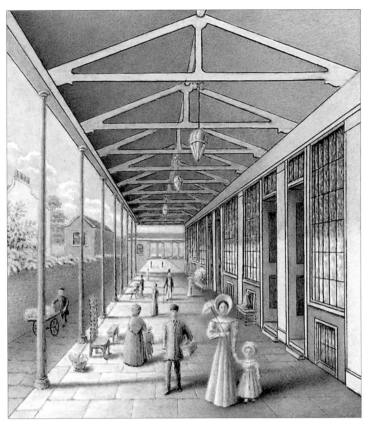

129 *An impression of the Market Arcade, 1840, by J.A. Probert. The shops sold books, millinery and other fancy goods, while poultry, meat and vegetables could be purchased from the market beyond.*

site of the former Albion Brewery in Gloucester Road. Thursday is still market day in Cheltenham and a further reminder is a set of three brass rods still visible in the path at the south-east corner of the church. These were once used to measure lengths of rope and cloth when the market was the retail centre of Cheltenham. Fairs, which for centuries had provided opportunities for hiring labour, continued to be held in the High Street throughout the 19th century. In his 1816 *Guide to Cheltenham* Griffiths described them as 'the crowding together of rustic lads and Bond Street beaux – of rural lasses and London belles'. An entry in the Christ Church Boys' School logbook dated 6 October 1864 shows their popularity: 'Cheltenham Mop Fair – only 38 [out of a possible 170] present at school today'.

The first major commercial development off the High Street was the Colonnade, which opened in 1791 with six shops. It led towards the future Promenade where commercial development began in 1826 at 3 Promenade Villas with the opening of Cavendish House Silk Mercery Establishment, Cheltenham's oldest department store. Opened by Clark and Debenham it expanded under several changes of ownership, finally joining House of Fraser in July 1975. Also in the Promenade is the jeweller's shop of Martin & Co. In 1822 Samuel Martin opened a branch of his silversmith's business in the High Street. The firm had moved to the present Promenade site by 1838 when appointed 'Goldsmiths in Ordinary' to Queen Victoria. Martin's supplied the first Cheltenham Gold Cup of 1823 and has held the permanent

use, first, as a solicitors' office, and then a Public Office where the magistrates held their thrice-weekly sessions. The Town Clock projected from the upper storey from 1827-1958 and the building was a Woolworth's store from 1915-60. It was demolished following a fire in 1969.

Lord Sherborne built a new Market House with an arcade of shops in 1823, on a site north of the High Street, adjoining Gardner's Brewery. The market declined in importance during the 1830s and 1840s with the increase in the number of shops and was closed in 1867, when the Arcade was replaced by Bennington Street, and the Centre Stone marked on the corner property, now a jeweller's. In 1876 the market re-opened on the

130 *George's Ltd, Bakers and Confectioners, High Street, 1901. Following her visit to Cheltenham in 1897, the Princess of Wales requested George's recipe for their vanilla biscuits, enhancing their already established reputation.*

contract to supply the Gold Cup, with other racing trophies, since 1933.

Many other Cheltenham shops and businesses traded for over a century. George's Ltd was founded *c.*1800 by David George, a pastry cook and confectioner, and was in business until 1940 with branches in Worcester, Cardiff, Malvern and Weston-super-Mare. David George is also credited with inventing the 'Dripper', a local favourite. Another long-lived firm was Thomas Plant & Co., established as a hatter's *c.*1823 by brothers Thomas and Edward Plant. It became a family-run school outfitter's that the Jewell family took over in 1901. It closed in 1999 after 176 years of trading.

One innovative firm in the town was Cheltine Foods, established in 1891 by T.E. Whitaker. The company specialised in food for diabetics, invalids and children and products included the Chelax digestive biscuit, which incorporated spa water in the recipe. The firm moved to Chester Walk in 1901 and ceased production in 1973.

Cheltenham has a long tradition of fine craftsmanship. James Hill was a Cheltenham-based master mason who specialised in Gothic church repairs. In 1675, with Francis Jones of Hasfield, he rebuilt the nave of Newent church, which had collapsed the previous year. In 1686, working with Francis Reeve, James Hill rebuilt

131 *Tewkesbury Abbey, c.1846, showing the fine west window rebuilt by James Hill of Cheltenham in 1686. Restoration work on the window was completed in 2004 at a cost of £250,000.*

132 *William Giles Brown (right) with his father, James, in 1873 working on the conversion of the Cambray Spa into the Cambray Turkish Baths. Both sculptors worked on the Houses of Parliament.*

the great west window at Tewkesbury Abbey, its medieval predecessor having been destroyed in a gale in 1661. In 1700 Hill rebuilt the central tower of Bishops Cleeve church, which had collapsed in 1696. The vestry minutes record his work in Cheltenham, where in 1693 'was the steeple of Cheltenham repayred from the upper hole to the top by James Hill'. He died in early 1734 and his probate inventory included 'grave stones and other stones in the yard', and recorded that he was owed over £300. Money was due 'for work done on Leckhampton Church' and from the 'Overseers of the Highways for Cheltenham, 1731'. He was owed a large sum by William Norwood, implying he had worked on Leckhampton Court, perhaps on the replacement of the north wing, which had been destroyed by fire in 1732. The largest sum was owed by Sir John Guise, who may have employed James Hill to work on Rendcomb Park or Elmore Court.

A number of stonemasons worked in Cheltenham during the 19th century, including George Lewis who produced a vast quantity of fine tombs and monuments before his death in 1868. James Brown, a stone carver of some renown, won the contract to carve the caryatids in Montpellier. His son William Giles, born c.1828, no doubt served his apprenticeship working on these contracts with his father. R.L. Boulton & Sons, a firm of ecclesiastical sculptors, began in London, with branches in Birmingham and Worcester. Richard Lockwood Boulton centralised the business in Cheltenham c.1866, and the firm led the country in the production of stone church furnishings. A fine example of their work is the huge stone reredos in the Cheltenham College Chapel, carved to the design of H.A. Prothero. The Bath Road premises closed in 1972.

Cheltenham's craftsmen produced excellent ornamental ironwork. The firm of R.E. & C. Marshall manufactured a variety of ironwork from 1822-1954, initially in the High Street, and then from premises in Royal Well Lane. Examples of Marshall's work include the railings outside Beech House, St James' Square, formerly the family home, and the chancel screen in St Philip and St James' Church. William Letheren began winning prizes for his art ironwork while managing Cormell's Lansdown Iron Works. In 1867 he won a Society of Arts competition with a wrought-iron screen, acquired for the nation by the Victoria & Albert Museum. At the time he was described as 'the greatest art ironworker in England', and he set

133 *Highbridge, Malvern Road, built by James Brown in 1856-7 to display his stone-carving skills. He lived in the adjoining house, which he also built, and let this one to provide a steady income for his family. (Photograph by Lisa Lavery.)*

up his own business, the Vulcan Iron Works, next door to Cormell's at Lansdown. In 1886 he was elected an Associate of the Society of Architects in recognition of his efforts in 'raising the standard of Art-work in metal, both ecclesiastical and domestic'. The Vulcan Iron Works closed in 1906. Another prize-winner was Charles William Hancock, awarded a silver medal at the 1908 Crystal Palace Industrial Exhibition for a wrought-iron panel, currently in the Cheltenham museum.

Cheltenham histories and guides have often stated that there was no heavy industry in the town. However, some substantial manufacturing

134 *Ornamental ironwork in one of the Montpellier Street entrance lobbies to the Ladies' College. It was made by William Letheren to the designs of architect Henry Allen Prothero in 1893-4. (Photograph by Lisa Lavery.)*

135 *The Bath Road entrance gates to Sandford Park, made by Charles William Hancock at his Bennington Street workshop in 1928.*

was carried out in Cheltenham, much of it now forgotten, possibly as it was not in keeping with the conscious promotion of the town's 'retired colonels' image. The arrival of the railway in 1840 facilitated heavier manufacture and by 1850 Shackleford's Carriage Works was established in Albion Street. During the 1850s the works expanded to produce railway carriages, trucks and horseboxes for the Great Western Railway. The noise and smoke nuisance drew constant complaints from the town, but in 1857 the firm acquired a site next to the GWR St James' Station. A large contract for Post Office railway carriages was completed in 1861 and by 1864 the annual wages bill reached £20,000 for about 400 men. During the 1860s Shackleford's went into partnership with a Swansea firm, becoming the Cheltenham & Swansea Wagon Co. In 1869 the Cheltenham branch was closed and the work transferred to Swansea.

In 1875 Messrs Vernon & Ewens set up the Central Iron Works on the site of Gibbs' (formerly

136 *A completed railway carriage being towed from Shackleford's Carriage Works to join the Great Western Railway.*

137 *Weyman & Hitchcock's Trusty Oil Engine Works,* c.1899. *The building in the centre foreground is the Vulcan Iron Works that can still be seen beside the railway, although much altered.*

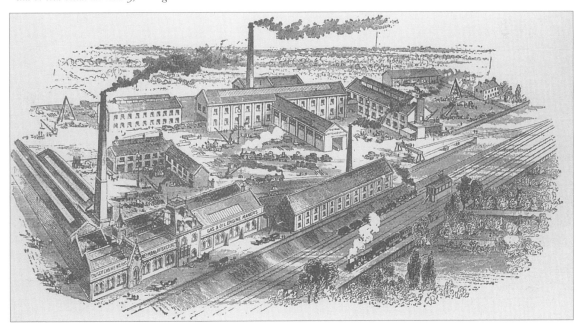

138 *A Trusty oil engine, c.1890s, one of only a handful known to survive, restored by Tim Macaire of North Devon by 2004. This is the only one in the world known to be in running order. A Trusty gas engine, undergoing restoration, is in the background.*

139 *Woodcarving studio at Sunningend, c.1923, shortly after the death of one of Martyn's greatest carvers, Harry Arthur Dean, whose craftsmanship was considered comparable with that of Grinling Gibbons. A fine example of his work is the 1907 Myers memorial in the Cheltenham College Chapel. Harry Dean's son is second from left in this photograph.*

140 *H.H. Martyn & Co., Sunningend, 1920s, looking east. Rowanfield Road is in the foreground bordered by market gardens, many of which had been run by the same families for generations. The site of Alstone Lawn is at the top left, before the building of Pates Avenue in 1933 to house families displaced by the Swindon Place clearance scheme.*

Cormell's) Lansdown Iron Works. In September 1876 the firm won the ironwork contract for the proposed Winter Gardens, Imperial Square, designed by J.T. Darby. The ironworks employed nearly 300 men, with an iron foundry, a steam joinery shop and a Tweddle's patent hydraulic riveting machine by Fielding & Platt of Gloucester. The firm had a joinery branch at Plymouth employing 150, and central offices at Westminster Chambers employing architects and draughtsmen. By 1880 the Cheltenham works had completed contracts which included ironwork for many new GWR stations and bridges, a large ship-building works at Pennar, a pier and pontoon at Tranmere on the Mersey, plus iron window-frames for the model estate at Petworth. Work in preparation

included a battery for the War Department on Maker Heights, Mount Edgecumbe. In 1882 Vernon & Ewens won an £80,000 contract to build the new Hammersmith suspension bridge over the Thames, designed by Sir Joseph Bazalgette. The casting for this used 1,000 tons of steel and 2-300 tons of ornamental cast-iron work. By 1890 the company had folded and the site was used briefly by Meats, Peake & Co. as the Central Engineering Works, for agricultural machinery repairs, before their removal to Montpellier.

In 1895 the site of the former Central Iron Works was considered by the entrepreneur Henry Lawson for premises to manufacture motor cars, but eventually he settled on Coventry as the place to expand the motor industry. Instead Weyman &

Hitchcock's Trusty Oil Engine Works took over the Lansdown site, encouraged by Mr Marshall and R.A. Lister of Dursley, who became company chairman. The firm had taken up the patents of the motoring pioneer, John Henry Knight, and by July 1895 they proudly reported that they had reduced the starting time of their oil engine from 55 minutes to only seven. The Trusty engine won many awards around the world, including a Gold Medal at the Chicago World's Fair in 1893. Following amalgamation in 1900, the firm became the Shillingford Engineering Co. Ltd at the Trusty Engine Works, but was in financial difficulties a few years later. It was eventually bought by Messrs Frederick Avens & Co. and transferred to Stroud.

The next firm to be established at Lansdown was that of H.H. Martyn & Co. Herbert Henry Martyn came to Cheltenham c.1866 to work for R.L. Boulton & Sons. He and another Boulton's stonecarver, E.A. Emms, left in 1874, setting up in partnership as monumental masons. In February 1888 Martyn establish H.H. Martyn and Co., with his son Alfred W. Martyn, at Sunningend, a house on the corner of the High Street and College Road. By 1900 Martyns had diversified into all aspects of architectural work, including large-scale bronze casting, decorative plaster, furniture and stained glass, supported by drawing and design offices. In 1908 the firm took over the former Trusty Engine Works and William Letheren's Vulcan Iron Works at Lansdown, renaming the site Sunningend. Martyn's reputation for fine quality attracted many craftsmen, both locally and from as far afield as Italy. The highly skilled Thomas Letheren, with other expert craftsmen from his father's old firm, worked in Martyn's ironwork department, housed in the original Vulcan Iron Works building. The craftsmen at Martyns had increased from 200 in 1905 to 1,000 by 1920.

Charles William Hancock joined the ironwork department as a manager and executed Martyn's first large-scale commission, the Marble Arch Cumberland Screen and Gates. These gates were removed from London in 1959; some rusted away in a Salford yard while some reputedly stand at a park entrance in Saskatchewan. Martyns went on to make decorative interiors for most of the world's great ocean liners, including the *Titanic, Lusitania, Queen Mary, Queen Elizabeth*, SS *Canberra* and *QE2*. During the 1920s Wolseley cars were produced and a Martyn scooter, the Unibus. Other work included the Whitehall Cenotaph, extensive war damage restoration in the House of Commons, including the Speaker's Chair and Dispatch Boxes, the St Paul's Cathedral pulpit and Robert the Bruce at Bannockburn. In 1934 H.H. Martyn & Co. became part of the Maple Group, who closed the company in 1971 after decades of international renown for fine craftsmanship.

ELEVEN

The Twentieth Century and Beyond

Britain declared war on Germany on 12 August 1914 and by the end of that month many patriotic young men were joining Kitchener's 'New Army' at the newly opened recruiting office near Alstone Baths, Great Western Road. By October over 1,400 had volunteered, with long lists of recruits being published in local newspapers. More than 300 men from the 1st Gloucestershire Royal Engineer Volunteers, disbanded in 1908, rejoined as regulars in the Royal Engineers in early 1915. as many as one in four of the 6-7,000 Cheltenham men who joined the 'war to end all wars' did not return. Those left behind supported the war effort by organising fund-raising events and knitting comforts for the troops. The first Red Cross Voluntary Aid Detachment (VAD) Hospital was opened at New Court, Lansdown Road with only 12 hours' notice in October 1914. Seven further VAD Hospitals, including those at the Racecourse, *Moorend Park Hotel* and the Ladies' College, opened over the next four years for British and foreign wounded. Nursing courses were run at the Technical School in St Margaret's Road and at the Town Hall.

Following wartime directives, H.H. Martyn & Co. utilised the woodworking skills of its craftsmen to make propellers, aircraft wings and fuselages. In 1916 about 1,000 extra workers, mostly women, produced aircraft in shadow factories, including the Winter Gardens where Bristol Fighter Aircraft were made. In 1917 A.W. Martyn conceived a plan to found the Gloucestershire Aircraft Company (later Gloster Aircraft Company or GAC) using Martyn's facilities and workforce, combined with contracts through the Aircraft Manufacturing Co. of Hendon. This joint employment of Martyns and GAC enabled both to survive the disastrous post-war period. By 1918 GAC was producing 45 fighter aircraft weekly, but as their aim was high-speed flight they employed Henry Folland, who had designed the SE5. Folland's designs won many air races and GAC's Schneider Trophy entries won two World Speed Records.

In 1925 A.W. Martyn boldly decided to separate the two companies, setting up GAC on a 200-acre site at Hucclecote where hangars already existed. In 1934 Hawker Aircraft acquired GAC, retaining their name however, and GAC produced fighters for the RAF between the wars. During the Second World War GAC produced 2,750 Hawker Hurricanes, 3,300 Typhoons and 600 Albemarle twin-engined aircraft. Designs included the allied first jet aircraft, the E28/29, with Frank Whittle's engine, and the Gloster Meteor Jet fighter, which took her maiden flight in spring 1941. Another GAC design, the Gloster Javelin, was a leader in delta wing technology, and 302 were produced at Hucclecote. In 1955 government policy reduced the demand for fighter aircraft, compelling GAC to turn to products as diverse as vending machines and fire engines, but in 1963 the last plane, a Gloster Javelin, flew out of Hucclecote and the site became a trading estate.

141 *A group of men from the 10th Gloucestershire Regiment with families and friends at the Midland Railway Station, Lansdown, returning to their Headquarters on 3 August 1915 after their final leave.*

Cheltenham people once again rallied at the outbreak of war in September 1939, raising funds for tanks, warships and Hurricane fighter planes, 'digging for victory' in gardens and playing fields, and recycling household waste. Scrap metal, salvaged to help the war effort, included the two cannon captured at the Battle of Sebastapol in 1855, that had stood outside the *Queen's Hotel*, and the First World War tank once prominently displayed in Montpellier Gardens. Local propaganda emphasised how much tidier the town would look without the clutter of railings and almost all were removed, ostensibly salvaged for reuse but most being simply dumped. One casualty of war was the Winter Gardens building which had provided a venue for various leisure activities, including roller-skating, since 1878. Expensive to maintain, it became something of a white elephant and was demolished in 1940-3, supposedly because it might attract enemy bombers.

Local people felt the direct effects of war when Cheltenham became a target for German air raids. The worst bombing took place on the night of 11 December 1940 when approximately 2,000 incendiary bombs and over 100 high explosives were dropped, killing 23 people and making 600 homeless. The greatest devastation occurred when a bomb hit the railway embankment at the end of Stoneville Street, killing ten people and destroying half the houses. A gasholder at the adjacent gasworks and part of the nearby Sunningend Works were also hit. St Margaret's Villa, the Black and White coach station's ticket office since 1931, was destroyed that night, as was Pilley Bridge, Leckhampton, the last war-damaged bridge in the country to be repaired, ten years later.

Two Cheltenham men had a significant role in the offensive against Germany. Arthur Travers Harris (1892-1984), born in Cheltenham, became Commander-in-Chief, Bomber Command RAF from 1942-5. Under his command 1,000 bomber raids were launched on Germany, resulting in the systematic destruction of German cities, in the belief that aerial bombardment alone would

142 *The production line for the Meteor VIII at the Gloster Aircraft Company, Hucclecote, in March 1951. The Meteor was built at the factory for 12 years, with variants that were sold to armed forces in the UK and exported to 14 other countries. The final Meteor left GAC on 9 April 1954.*

143 *Bomb damage in Brunswick Street, caused in the morning of 27 July 1942 when Cheltenham's second most serious air raid took place. Six houses were totally demolished, 11 people were killed and 25 were injured. (Photograph courtesy of the* Gloucestershire Echo.*)*

defeat the enemy. This earned him the nickname of 'Bomber Harris' but involved appalling losses in aircraft and crew. The other local man was Sqn Leader R.W. Reynolds, of Orrisdale Terrace, Regent Street, who led the first daylight raid on Berlin.

The war brought a large influx of people to the town, including child evacuees from London and Birmingham, Polish airmen and Italian prisoners of war. Many buildings were commandeered, including Montpellier Rotunda which was used as an ammunition store. The American Forces of Supply arrived in 1943, occupying single-storey buildings at Benhall and Oakley (later used by

---

Passenger Flights and Great Aviation Display

AT

BENHALL FARM,

GLOUCESTER ROAD, CHELTENHAM,

From March 18th to 29th Inclusive.

PASSENGER FLIGHTS DAILY

At 5/-, 10/-, 15/-, and £1,

Looping the Loop 15s.

Other Stunts by arrangement. We guarantee satisfaction or money refunded. Many thousands of passengers have flown with us without a single complaint.—"Be up-to-date and Aviate."

---

144 *The rapid developments in aviation in the early part of the century captured everybody's imagination, shown by this advertisement from the* Cheltenham Chronicle and Gloucestershire Graphic *of 1926. Before the growth of the suburbs, air displays could be held much nearer the centre of town.*

GCHQ). The *Queen's Hotel* became an American Services Club and Pittville Pump Room was requisitioned as a US storage depot. Glenn Miller and Bob Hope entertained the US troops and Joe Louis, world heavyweight boxing champion, gave an exhibition bout to American GIs and uniformed men, including the Home Guard and boy scouts. Norman Wisdom was billeted at the *Moray Hotel* (now the *Carlton*) with the Royal Corps of Signals from 1943-5. He formed a dance band, which played locally, and after a charity concert at the Town Hall actor Rex Harrison encouraged him to become an entertainer.

In January 1929 George Dowty, a young draughtsman at GAC, was granted a full patent on his internally sprung landing-wheel design. In 1931, persuaded by an article Dowty had written about his design, a Japanese company ordered six wheels. Dowty quit GAC and manufactured the wheels himself in a loft at 10 Lansdown Terrace Lane. By 1935 the tiny workspace and severe lack of finance was crippling the company, and Dowty's search for financial backing was proving fruitless, or involved becoming an employee again. He approached his former employer, A.W. Martyn, who recognised the potential of Dowty's innovative skills and business acumen. Martyn immediately arranged a £3,000 guarantee in the company's bank account, followed by a £30,000 cash injection for expansion, which included the purchase of Arle Court following refusal of planning permission for a Cheltenham factory.

In just four years Dowty's had orders worth £10 million and had opened two more factories, in Canada and the USA. During the Second World War one million hydraulic units and 87,000 retractable undercarriages were made for numerous aircraft including Lancasters, Hurricanes, Meteors and the Gloster/Whittle Jet. By the mid-1950s the Dowty Group, comprising 25 companies world wide, was by far the largest European manufacturer

145 *The GCHQ site at Benhall, with the single-storey wartime buildings in the foreground, the 1980s multi-storey block in the centre, and the 'Doughnut', which was fully occupied by late 2004.*

of aircraft equipment. George Dowty became an Honorary Freeman of the Borough in 1955 and in 1956 received a knighthood. In 1992 the TI Group bought the Dowty Group for £504 million and sold off parts of the business, including the original undercarriage division, bought by the French aerospace group Snecma in 1997.

Dowtys, GAC and other local aviation companies tested their new developments on planes flown from the municipal airport at Staverton, both during and after the war. In 1937 the Air Ministry commandeered Staverton airport, opened in 1934, and set up No. 31 Elementary and Reserve Flying Training School. During the war allied airmen were given basic practical and theoretical training at RAF Staverton before moving to RAF stations elsewhere. Many RAF and WAAF ground crew were also trained at the nearby No. 4 School of Technical Training, Innsworth. Staverton was not re-opened for civilian use until 1952.

In 1939 S. Smith & Sons Ltd, a London-based clock and watch company that had manufactured parts including altimeters for the earliest First World War aeroplanes, purchased 300 acres at Kaytes Farm, Bishops Cleeve. Reputedly, Smiths managing director chose the site because of its proximity to the racecourse. The first factory, making special aviation instruments, was completed in 1940 and immediately camouflaged. Output from the company during the Second World War included one and a half million speedometers and mileage counters, ten million aircraft instruments and four million clocks. In 1966 Smiths Industries Ltd achieved international recognition when a Trident test aircraft became the first civilian airliner to land in thick fog under full automatic control, using a Smiths autopilot. Smiths acquired Lear Siegler Holdings Corp., a major US avionics manufacturer, in 1986 and aerospace became Smiths core business. The firm merged with the TI Group, Dowtys' parent company, in December

2000, bringing together two powerful players in the industry, and Smiths Aerospace was officially launched at the Paris Air Show in 2001.

Large-scale car production almost ceased during the Second World War, with British and German manufacturers making utility items for the war effort. However, in 1943 the aeronautical engineer Sir Roy Fedden, Special Technical Advisor to the Ministry of Aircraft Production, managed to obtain sanction to develop a prototype vehicle, hoping it would become a people's car similar to the Volkswagen. He leased Benton House, The Park from Dowty Engineering and with his design team produced the rear-engined 1.EX. On 6 December 1946 it was successfully tested by Alec Caine at the Black & White Motorways yard, St Margaret's Road. On a later test run the drivers met an unusual car in a quiet Cotswold lane. Both parties inspected each other's vehicles, wordlessly, before driving on. The strange car was the prototype Morris Minor, driven by (Sir) Alec Issigonis. Regrettably, Fedden's rear-engined car

was continually beset by stability problems and the project was abandoned in 1947.

Government Communications Headquarters (GCHQ) moved from Bletchley Park, Buckinghamshire, to sites at Oakley and Benhall in 1952. For years the work of the 'Foreign Office', as it was known locally, was a mystery to most people in Cheltenham. However, in 1982 the trial of Geoffrey Prime, a GCHQ linguist who had been spying for the Russians, raised public awareness and in 1983 the Department's role was acknowledged publicly for the first time. The banning of Trade Unions at GCHQ from 1984-97 aroused further publicity and considerable debate. GCHQ's Signals Intelligence work has provided information to support government decision-making on international issues, such as the Suez Crisis and the Gulf War. Increasingly intelligence has also been used to combat terrorism and to detect and prevent serious crime. The Communications Electronic Security Group (CESG) within GCHQ has helped protect government communication and information systems, and national infrastructure from hackers and other threats. In 2000 the government approved plans for a new purpose-built £337 million headquarters for GCHQ, to replace 50 largely outdated buildings spread over the two sites. GCHQ has become the biggest employer in Gloucestershire, with one of the largest computer complexes in Europe.

146 *The interior of the GCHQ 'Doughnut' showing the glass roof, open-plan office space and palm trees. The award-winning building has been designed to be energy-efficient and environmentally friendly, and a high proportion of the furniture was made from recycled materials.*

Demand for motor cars in the early 20th century encouraged local carriage builders to diversify into car bodywork. Alfred Miles included a model called the 'Doctor's Special' in his range in 1910. After the First World War

147 *The motor car was beginning to have an impact on Cheltenham when the first filling station at Westal Green was opened in 1928. It was designed for the garage proprietor, Mr O. Goulding, by Clough Williams-Ellis of Portmeirion fame.*

In 1921 Cecil Gardner set up Cheltenham Caravans Ltd, at first building motor homes on car chassis. Following the Second World War the firm constructed caravans using military surplus, including spitfire wheels, and pioneered the use of fibreglass. In 1926 George Readings established the Black & White Coach Company at the former Diamond Laundry premises, Charlton Kings, initially touring around Cheltenham but soon running daily return journeys to London. Readings introduced many innovations, including on-board toilets and the sale of tickets through local retail outlets. By the late 1920s three million coach passengers passed through the town annually. Cheltenham remained a national

touring by car, coach or train became increasingly popular and Cheltenham was being advertised as the 'Centre for the Cotswolds' by the late 1920s.

148 *On 28 December 1929 the* Cheltenham Chronicle and Gloucestershire Graphic *reported that, 'A young lady dressed as Dick Turpin, riding a pony, and holding a pistol, has been holding up Black and White Coaches at Puesdown and giving Christmas cards to the passengers.'*

149 *Sandford Lido soon after its opening in 1935. Designed by the borough engineer, Gilbert Gould Marsland, it is one of the few swimming pools of its type remaining in the country.*

150 *Dragon Boat Racing on Pittville Lake, 2003. This event celebrated the 40th anniversary of the Samaritans in Cheltenham and raised over £11,000. Pittville Park has long been a venue for festival events and other entertainments. (Photograph by Dave Martin.)*

interchange for long-distance coach travel until business declined after the M5 opened in 1970.

Twentieth-century transport innovations made access to other parts of the country easy and affordable, giving everybody the opportunity to travel. Guidebooks were needed for the increasing number of tourists, and a Cheltenham entrepreneur, Ed Burrow, seized this opportunity. Already established as an illustrator, he set up his own publishing firm, Ed. J. Burrow & Co. Ltd, in 1900 at St John's Lodge, Hewlett Road. Burrow's first commission was for a Cheltenham guidebook, and the firm went on to produce guides for the whole country, including the popular *Dunlop Guide* series. In 1924 Burrow opened an 'All for Travel Depot' in London which, besides guidebooks, offered European booking facilities, maps, travel equipment and information on local services across the country. In 1974 the firm was moved to London by its controlling group, Pyramid Publishers.

As the 20th century progressed, the Town Council became increasingly involved in providing recreational facilities. As early as 1887 Alstone Baths, the town's first municipal swimming baths, had opened beside Upper Alstone Mill. The Lido, a fashionable open-air swimming pool, opened in Sandford Park in 1935 on a former allotment site. Sandford Park itself, opened in 1928, is one of the many green spaces made available to the town by the Council since incorporation in 1876. In 1902 the Council opened the former Hampton's Gardens, Albion Street, as an Athletic Ground and many more recreation grounds were created during the 20th century, including the Prince of Wales Stadium, opened at Pittville in 1981.

At one time Cheltenham had seven cinemas, including the Gaumont (now the Odeon), built on the site of Highbury Chapel in 1933. The Theatre and Opera House (later the Everyman) also showed films, including the town's first 'talkie', *Bulldog Drummond* starring Ronald Coleman, in

1929. After the Second World War Cheltenham became known for its festivals, echoing the aims of the Literary and Philosophical Institution of the previous century, but this time with music, literature and science accessible to all. Benjamin Britten, William Walton and Arthur Bliss conducted their own work in front of culture-hungry audiences at the first Cheltenham Music Festival, held just three weeks after war ended. The event has always attracted top-class musicians, including opera singer José Carreras who performed at Cheltenham Racecourse in 2003. The Fringe Festival, run alongside the Music Festival, has included Picnic in the Park, a popular free family event held in front of Pittville Pump Room. The Cheltenham International Jazz Festival was begun in 1996, attracting some of the biggest names in jazz, and an annual Folk Festival has been successful.

151 *Jimi Hendrix, Blue Moon Club, 1965, taken by Michael Charity, the only photographer at the event. Hendrix honoured his contract to play at the club, which had been agreed shortly before his sudden rise to fame.*

152 *A Cheltenham slum dwelling, 1920s. Some of the town's poorest residents inhabited streets and courts off Swindon Road, such as Swindon Place where 38 houses shared just three earth privies.*

The driving force behind Cheltenham's first Festival of Literature in 1949 was the well-known Tewkesbury author John Moore. Actor Ralph Richardson, who had lived in Tivoli Road until the age of five, launched the Festival, the first of its kind in the country, and poet Cecil Day Lewis read a selection of contemporary verse. Day Lewis continued to support the event until his death in 1972. The Festival has grown to include over 250 events each October and recently a second Festival of Literature was introduced in the Spring. All previous Festival attendance records were broken in March 2004 when an audience of 1,700 listened to Dame Judi Dench at the racecourse's new Centaur Complex. Cheltenham has also hosted an annual Science Festival since 2002, featuring well-known figures from the fields of both academic and popular science.

The late 1950s saw the development of a thriving music scene, with a large student population frequenting jazz venues such as the *Star* (Regent Street) and the Waikiki Club (Montpellier). One of the most popular haunts was the basement of 38 Priory Street, a jazz café run by Jane Philby.

Pop replaced jazz in the early 1960s, with visitors such as Cliff Richard and the Shadows, Dusty Springfield and Herman's Hermits. In November 1963 the Beatles gave two short performances to hordes of screaming fans at the Odeon, and stayed at the *Savoy Hotel*, Montpellier (now *Hotel Kandinsky*). Within two weeks the band topped the charts with *I Wanna Hold Your Hand* and *She Loves You*. The Rolling Stones also played at the Odeon in September 1964. The band's Cheltenham-born guitarist, Brian Jones, had attended Dean Close Junior School and Cheltenham Grammar School and had trained as a bus conductor at the Bristol Omnibus Tramway Club, Royal Well. Following Brian's death in 1969 his grave in Cheltenham Cemetery became a site of pilgrimage for his fans. Rock guitarist Jimi Hendrix played at the Blue Moon Club, above Burton's the tailor in the High Street, in 1965, as did The Who and Elton John.

Despite its air of respectability, Cheltenham continued to have areas of deprivation, particularly at the western end of the town. In 1919 the Town Council bought 115 acres at St Mark's, off Gloucester Road, for £10,500 and the first houses in Cheltenham's new 'Garden Suburb' were opened three years later. The Town Council set up a Slum Area Clearance Committee in 1924 and from 1929, when the Whaddon Farm estate was begun, rehousing programmes continued until the 1960s. Princess Elizabeth cut the first turf for one of the largest schemes, the Hesters Way Estate, in 1951, and 3,000 homes had been erected there by 1960. With Cheltenham's population reaching over 100,000 by the turn of the millennium, the suburbs have continued to expand on all sides of the borough.

153 Newly completed houses in Tennyson Road, 1925. In 1920 it was agreed that the roads in the new garden suburb of St Mark's should be named after English poets, only some of whom had connections with the town. The first ten houses were ready for occupation in January 1921.

154 'The Minotaur and the Hare' sculpture by Sophie Ryder aroused considerable controversy when it was first placed in the lower Promenade, but its supporters raised £50,000 to buy it for the town in 1997. Surprisingly, considering Cheltenham's heritage, history of craftsmanship and variety of public sculpture, the town has no permanent arts centre. (Photograph by Lisa Lavery.)

Many landmark buildings were demolished during the 1960s, such as the New Club (Promenade), the ancient Tinkler's Basket Shop and the 1889 Grammar School building (High Street), often to be replaced by featureless concrete retail units. Two decaying buildings miraculously escaped demolition: Pittville Pump Room was extensively refurbished, to be re-opened by the 7th Duke of Wellington in 1960; and Montpellier Rotunda, bought by Lloyds Bank in 1961 for £14,000, was also carefully restored. Speculative office building was at its height in the 1960s, boosted by central government initiatives to move business development out of London. Ironically the insensitive seven-storey Brewery Headquarters (1966) and the 13-storey Eagle Star Headquarters (1968) stand empty awaiting redevelopment. In 1972 the Cheltenham and

155 The Eagle Star tower block has dominated Cheltenham's skyline since 1968. Ironically, the Regency building dwarfed by it, Eagle Lodge, has taken on a new lease of life as a conference facility, while Eagle Tower struggles to find a new use in the new millennium. (Photograph by Lisa Lavery.)

Gloucester Building Society (founded at the *Belle Vue Hotel* in 1850) opened a new headquarters, complete with Barbara Hepworth sculpture, in Clarence Street. Cheltenham lost four of its five railway stations following Beeching's closure of the British Rail Western Regional line in 1962, the sites at Charlton Kings and Leckhampton becoming industrial estates. Although Malvern Road Station was demolished, the nearby engine shed became a warehouse for Travis Perkins, Gloucester Road, where the art nouveau letters GWR still grace the ironwork gates. The extensive St James' Station site remained empty for 40 years until the building of the Waitrose store in 2002.

In the early 1970s a change in national policy favoured the refurbishment of existing buildings and pressure from local groups such as the Cheltenham Society (later Cheltenham Civic Society) led to the rediscovery of the town's architectural heritage. A Conservation Area covering most of central Cheltenham was established in 1973 and grants were made available for upgrading domestic buildings. Prestige-conscious companies were attracted by the availability of large Regency and Georgian mansions for conversion to offices, such as Thirlestaine Hall, Chelsea Building Society Headquarters since 1973. The Daffodil cinema, Suffolk Parade, of 1922 with a unique Art Deco interior, was used as a furniture warehouse for many years following its closure, but sensitively converted to a restaurant in 1998. Arle Court, formerly Dowty Group Headquarters, became Cheltenham Film Studios in 1998 providing facilities outside London for media industries. Two misguided demolitions of the 1960s have been replaced in facsimile: Jenner's house in St George's Place (demolished 1969) was rebuilt with a replica façade in 1994; and the Priory (replaced by an unimaginative office block in 1967) was rebuilt as Wellington Place in 1998. Cheltenham remains well-known as a Regency town, despite regrettable planning decisions in the last century. As early as 1826 Fosbroke, commenting on the town's architecture, warned us to 'Guard this great charm of the place. Destroy it, and Cheltenham is no more.'

Further Reading

Adams, W.E., *Memoirs of a Social Atom* (1903, reprinted 1967)

Arlott, John, *100 Years of Gloucestershire Cricket* (date unknown)

Avery, Gillian, *Cheltenham Ladies* (2003)

Awdry, W. (ed.), *Industrial Archaeology in Gloucestershire* (1973)

Bancroft Judge, Rev. G.H., *The Origin and Progress of Wesleyan Methodism in the Cheltenham Circuit 1739-1912* (1912)

Beacham, Roger, *Cheltenham As It Was* (1976)

Bell, Arthur, *Tudor Foundation* (1974)

Bennett, Nicola, *Speaking Volumes: A History of the Cheltenham Festival of Literature* (1999)

Bick, David, *The Gloucester and Cheltenham Railway* (1968)

Bick, David, *Old Leckhampton* (1994)

Blake, Steven, *Cheltenham Churches and Chapels 773-1883* (1979)

Blake, Steven, *Cheltenham: A Pictorial History* (1996)

Blake, Steven, *Pittville, 1824-1860* (1988)

Blake, Steven, *Views of Cheltenham 1786-1860* (1984)

Blake, Steven and Beacham, Roger, *The Book of Cheltenham* (1982)

Bristol and Gloucestershire Archaeological Society, *Transactions* (1981-2002)

British Geological Survey, *British Regional Geology – Bristol and Gloucester Region* (3rd edn 1992)

Brooks, Robin, *The Story of Cheltenham* (2003)

Cant, Peter, *The History of the Cheltenham Archers 1857-1975* (c.1975)

Challinor, E.B., *The Story of St. Mary's College Cheltenham* (1968)

Charlton Kings Local History Society, *Britain in Old Photographs: Charlton Kings* (1999)

Chatwin, Amina, *Cheltenham's Ornamental Ironwork* (1974)

Charity, Michael, *Cheltenham People and Places 1960s to 1980s* (2001)

Cheltenham Annuaires and Directories, 1837-1975

Cheltenham The Garden Town of England (1901)

Cheltenham Guide Books, 1781-1982

Cheltenham Local History Society, *CLHS Journals* 1-20 (1983-2004)

Cheltenham Spa Campaign, *St George's Place* (1978)

Cobbett, William, *Rural Rides* (1821)

Dawes, Edwin A., *The Great Illusionists* (1979)

Denning, Anthony, *Theatre in the Cotswolds* (1993)

Devereux, D. and Sacker, G., *Leaving All That Was Dear: Cheltenham and the Great War* (1997)

Dreghorn, William, *Geology Explained in the Severn Vale and the Cotswolds* (1967)

Finberg, H.P.R. (ed.), *Gloucestershire Studies* (1957)

Fisher, Richard B., *Edward Jenner 1749-1823* (1991)

Fosbroke, T.D., *An Account of Cheltenham and its Vicinity* (1826)

Gill, Peter, *Cheltenham at War* (1994)

Gill, Peter, *Cheltenham Races* (1997)

Girling, M.A. and Hooper, L., Sir, *Dean Close School: The First 100 Years* (1986)

Gloucestershire Notes and Queries (1881-1914)

Gloucestershire Record Office, *Cheltenham Manor Court Books* (17th-19th centuries)

Goding, J, *Norman's History of Cheltenham* (1863)

Granville, A.B., *Spas of England & Principal Sea-bathing Places* (1841)

Hallett, Michael, *Professional Photographers in Cheltenham 1841-1914* (1986)

Hannam-Clarke, Theodore, *Drama in Gloucestershire* (1928)

Hart, Gwen, *A History of Cheltenham* (1965, reprinted 1981)

Heasman, Elaine, *Images of England: Cheltenham* (1998)

Heasman, Elaine, *Images of England: Cheltenham Vol. II* (2003)

Hembry, Phyllis, *British Spas from 1815 to the Present* (1997)

Hembry, Phyllis, *The English Spa 1560-1815, A Social History* (1990)

Herbert, Stephen and McKernan, Luke, *Who's Who of Victorian Cinema* (1996)

Hodsdon, James, *An Historical Gazetteer of Cheltenham* (1997)

Holst, Imogen, *Holst* (1972)

Humphris, E. and Willoughby, E.C., *At Cheltenham Spa* (1928)

James, Derek N., *Dowty and the Flying Machine* (1996)

James, Derek N., *The Flying Machine in Gloucestershire* (2003)

James, Derek, *Gloster Aircraft Company* (2000)

Jones, Anthea, *A Short History of the First Cheltenham Spa in Bayshill* (1988)

Lee, John, *A New Guide to Cheltenham and its Environs* (1843)

Little, Bryan, *Cheltenham* (1952)

Little, Bryan, *Cheltenham in Pictures* (1967)

Local Newspapers including: *Cheltenham Chronicle and Gloucestershire Graphic, Cheltenham Journal, Cheltenham Looker-On, Cheltenham Free Press, Cheltenham Examiner, Gloucestershire Echo*

Magee, D., *The History of the Cheltenham Croquet Club* (2004)

McCann, W.P. and Young, F., *Samuel Wilderspin and the Infant School Movement* (1982)

McNeile, R.F., *History of Dean Close School* (1966)

Mills, Stephen and Pierce, Riemer, *The Mills of Gloucestershire* (1989)

Morgan, M.C., *Cheltenham College: The First Hundred Years* (1968)

National Archives, *Cheltenham Manor Court Rolls* (14th-16th centuries)

O'Connor, David A., *The Hole in the Ground – the Story of the Battledown Brickworks* (2002)

Osmond, Stephen E., *A Chronology of Cheltenham 200BC to AD2000* (2000)

Pakenham, Simona, *Cheltenham, A Biography* (1971)

Pearce, Tim, *Then and Now, an Anniversary Celebration of Cheltenham College, 1841-1991* (1991)

Platts, A. and Hainton, G.H., *Education In Gloucestershire: A Short History* (1954)

Raikes, Elizabeth, *Dorothea Beale of Cheltenham* (1908)

Richardson, L., *A Handbook to the Geology of Cheltenham* (1904)

Rolt, L.T.C., *The Aeronauts* (1985)

Sacker, Graham, *Held in Honour, Cheltenham and The Second World War* (2000)

Sale, A.J.H. (ed.), *Cheltenham Probate Records 1660-1740* (1999)

Sampson, Aylwin, *They Lived Here in Cheltenham* (1981)

Sampson, Aylwin and Blake, Steven, *A Cheltenham Companion* (1993)

Saville, Alan, *Archaeology in Gloucestershire* (1984)

Stratford, Joseph, *Good and Great Men of Gloucestershire* (1860s)

Torode, Brian, *The Hebrew Community of Cheltenham, Gloucester and Stroud* (1989)

Trafford, R.S., *The Rev. Francis Close and the Founding of the Training Institution at Cheltenham 1845-78* (1997)

Verey, David, *The Buildings of England: Gloucestershire 2: The Vale and the Forest of Dean* (1970)

Verey, David, and Brooks, Alan, *The Buildings of England: Gloucestershire 2: The Vale and the Forest of Dean* (2002)

Verey, D. (ed.), *The Diary of a Cotswold Parson* (1978)

Waller, Jill, *A Chronology of Crime and Disorder in Cheltenham* (2004)

Waller, Jill, *A Chronology of Sickness & Health in Cheltenham* (2003)

Waller, Jill, *A Chronology of Trade & Industry in Cheltenham* (2002)

Whitaker, John, *The Best* (1985)

Whiting, Roger, *Cheltenham in Old Photographs* (1986)

Whiting, Roger, *Cheltenham in Old Photographs :A Second Selection* (1988)

Who's Who in Cheltenham (1910)

Williams, G.A., *Williams' Guide to Cheltenham* (1824)

Wilson, D.M. and Elder, D.B., *Cheltenham in Antarctica: The Life of Edward Wilson* (2000)

Index

References which relate to illustrations only are given in **bold**.

Map of Cheltenham published 1824 by
G.A. Williams, Librarian.

Charlton to Westall

Sandford to Westall

THE RIVER CHELT

Original
Chalybeate
Spa

Montpellier Rides

New Walks

Rides Walk

HIGH STREET

Berkley Street

Witcomb Place

Grove Terrace

Old Road to Prestbury

Old Road to Prestbury

Toll Bar

Road from Hewlett's

MAP
OF
CHELTENHAM.

Published, 1824. by
G.A. WILLIAMS.
Librarian Cheltenham.